N6

SEATTLE CITY
OF LITERATURE

SEATTLE

CITY OF

LITERATURE

REFLECTIONS FROM
A COMMUNITY OF WRITERS

ED. RYAN BOUDINOT

SASQUATCH BOOKS
SEATTLE

Printed in the United States of America

Published by Sasquatch Books
19 18 17 16 15   9 8 7 6 5 4 3 2 1

Editor: Hannah Elnan
Production editor: Emma Reh
Design: Anna Goldstein
Map illustrator: Teresa Grasseschi
Copyeditor: Elizabeth Johnson

Library of Congress Cataloging-in-Publication
Data is available.

ISBN: 978-1-57061-986-1

Sasquatch Books
1904 Third Avenue, Suite 710
Seattle, WA 98101
(206) 467-4300
www.sasquatchbooks.com
custserv@sasquatchbooks.com

Certified Chain of Custody
SUSTAINABLE   Promoting Sustainable Forestry
FORESTRY
INITIATIVE   www.sfiprogram.org
               SFI-01268

SFI label applies to the text stock

CONTENTS

SEATTLE, CREATIVE CITY

BY RYAN BOUDINOT

I s Seattle a city of literature? Ask those of us who live for the city's many independent bookstores, libraries, classes, presses, journals, literary arts organizations, readings, and book-related events, and you'll get an emphatic *yes*. This is one of the best cities in America—if not *the* best city—for book lovers, and we can point to an annual national poll to back up the claim.[1] But those of us who write here know in our bones that this is a city with rare devotion to the written word. For this anthology, a representative selection of the city's writers and book lovers were invited to share their favorite stories of literary Seattle. I told the contributors I wanted to hear the kinds of stories they'd tell in a bar, among their writer friends, after the third round. Judging by some of the submissions I received, some of the writers took this directive more literally than others.

But to understand Seattle as a place for readers, writers, and books, it's helpful to situate literature within the context of a city where many forms of creative expression flourish and influence one another. Artists—whether they're musicians, dancers, actors, filmmakers, visual artists, etc.—thrive here.

---

[1] As of this writing, Central Connecticut State University, which conducts the America's Most Literate Cities poll, has ranked Seattle as number one or number two every year since the poll started.

If you lived in the Pacific Northwest prior to the World Wide Web, it was easy to assume that the world at large didn't know this corner of the country existed. The cultural umbilical cords that originate in New York and Los Angeles sent their movies, TV shows, bands, and books our way, and we devoured what was served. I have fond memories of chopping wood in a Skagit Valley sheep pasture while blasting N.W.A.'s *Straight Outta Compton* on a boom box, and reading about the coked-up demimonde of Jay McInerney's *Bright Lights, Big City* while on a school bus passing tulip fields.

For much of the Northwest's cultural history, our purpose seemed to be that of passive consumers of culture, or at best a farm team whose brightest artists (Frances Farmer, Jimi Hendrix, Merce Cunningham, et al) decamped for the country's "real" cultural production centers. When an artistic genius rose from the Pacific Northwest, he or she was quickly swallowed, like a comedian from neighboring Canada, by America's entertainment machine.

Pre-Internet, we were sort of left to our own devices here in the upper left corner. Once in a while, a news magazine would swoop in to explain us. *They sure do drink a lot of fancy coffee up there! What's with those salmon? Hey, look, software! It rains a lot!*

In the funky '80s, Tacoma-native Gary Larson produced *The Far Side*, the one-paneled masterpiece that shook up the *Garfield* orthodoxy of the inaptly named "funny pages." Raymond Carver, who grew up in Yakima, had started his long occupation of MFA program syllabi. The documentary *Streetwise*, about Seattle's homeless children, played on local TV with all the curse words intact, painting the city as an unforgiving concrete netherworld crawling with pederasts and drug dealers. The riotous comics of Matt Groening and Lynda Barry, both graduates of The Evergreen State College in Olympia, started appearing in alt weeklies and on office break-room bulletin boards.

In the early '90s, Washington State would show off its Douglas firs and dark secrets on national television with *Twin Peaks*, cocreated by David Lynch, who spent part of his childhood in Spokane.

Then God plugged a guitar into an amplifier. And there was a screech of feedback. And it was good. More to the point, it was *loud*.

The moment I realized that truly *cool* art could come from Seattle was when I dropped the needle on Mudhoney's self-titled LP. What impressed me most about that album, and about Mudhoney in general, was that they seemed utterly uninterested in impressing anybody. (During a free outdoor show at Seattle Center, lead singer Mark Arm declared, "Say what you will about Mudhoney—you get what you pay for.") They created snotty, aggressive, vulgar music in a garage somewhere, and they didn't seem to care what anybody thought. This attitude pervaded the scene. I bought as many tapes (yes, cassettes!) by local bands as I could afford. If the band lived in Seattle and the members all wore their hair past their nipples, I figured they were worth checking out. I had no clue what Soundgarden sounded like when I purchased *Ultramega OK*. I bought *Bleach* thinking that the name Nirvana really should have belonged to a more famous band.

What happened next, of course, is history well-preserved in Seattle's EMP Museum, or what I like to call the Museum of Twelve-Year-Old Boys' Bedrooms. Grunge changed popular music for the better, and while the plaid flannel and vintage distortion pedals got a lot of attention and occasional ridicule, there were three crucial elements of that music that provided a model for how artists in the Northwest might engage the world.

First, the lyrics. The wave of musicians that included Kurt Cobain, Kathleen Hanna, Chris Cornell, and Carrie Brownstein came into their own during a period when American popular music was, lyrically, pretty much the exact opposite of everything Bob Dylan has ever stood for. Thanks to Seattle bands, we went from "she's my cherry pie" to "raining icepicks on your steel shore" almost overnight. Grunge took the DIY ethos of Washington, DC's hardcore scene, kicked the misogyny out of metal, and added poetry. When Kurt Cobain lived on Pear Street in Olympia, it would take him just a couple minutes to walk to Counterpoint Books, a used bookstore owned by a curmudgeonly leftist with questionable shelving skills. It's here, I imagine, that Cobain encountered books by Thomas Pynchon and William S. Burroughs, whose prose informed his lyrics. This store, later sold to the original owner's daughter, would become Orca Books, where I worked for a time after college, and where I occasionally sold books to the members of Sleater-Kinney. I submit that the secret ingredient of the Northwest's late twentieth-century musical renaissance was prose.

With a much more diverse palette of lyrical content came an attitude shift toward those who were frequently marginalized by American popular music. The poodle-haired heteronormative rock god became instant self-parody the moment Kurt put on a dress. Women claimed more of their rightful place in rock music's canon, and, thanks largely to the Riot Grrl movement, launched the third wave of feminism, running Susan Faludi's sexual politics through

Marshall stacks. Homophobia became profoundly uncool. Those of us who frequented punk shows in the early '90s remember the vibe—supportive, self-reliant, open to experimentation, accepting of differences. These values bled into other artistic forms. I was among many young writers who took artistic cues from albums as much as books.

And it's clear that this reassertion of values wasn't fleeting. There's a straight (queer?) line from Cobain's "What else should I say? / Everyone is gay" to Seattle hip-hop giant Macklemore's "Same Love." The embryonic version of the newspaper that would become Seattle's *Stranger* featured an acerbic young sex advice columnist named Dan Savage, who answered letters addressed "Hey, Faggot." Decades later, as an author and the *Stranger*'s editorial director, Savage would launch the wildly viral It Gets Better Project to encourage and empower LGBT youth. Today, it's not a stretch to say he's one of the country's most respected civil rights leaders.

Sexual identity isn't the only arena in which Northwest art exerts its empathetic influence; we intend to get as much use out of the First Amendment as possible up here. Few have spoken more forcefully and eloquently about freedom of expression than Seattle's Sherman Alexie, whose National Book Award–winning *The Absolutely True Diary of a Part-Time Indian* and other works have landed him on banned books lists curated by the more ignorant of our country's school boards.

And while popular music from the Northwest introduced new literary values and a new conscience to rock and roll, it had just as profound an impact as a business model. Those of us who lived through that era remember wondering when, and to whom, Sub Pop would sell out. The indie record company, well fed by the expense accounts of major record labels throughout the early '90s, never took the bait. Many of us kept waiting for it to happen, but it never did. Sub Pop founders and Evergreen grads Jonathan Poneman and Bruce Pavitt took a look at that dollar bill dangling from the fishhook and shrugged, then went on to give us the Murder City Devils, the Shins, Shabazz Palaces, and many others.

I'm willing to argue that Sub Pop's resilience in the face of pressure to make a quick buck was the most important development in Pacific Northwest art since those transcendentalist Northwest School painters tripped out on magic mushrooms. The refusal to outsource the cultural production capacity of our city was an expression of faith. Faith that what we have here is sophisticated enough to sustain itself and reward artists as long as we're so moved by the muses. Faith that we can create serious art of global reach right here. Faith that we're more than qualified to assume responsibility for a significant sector of the country's creative economy.

Which brings us back to books. As author and advocate of Pacific Northwest literature Nick O'Connell once put it, the history of writers in Seattle has largely been the history of what New York editors think of Seattle. The anthology you're holding was compiled, in part, to change that.

Seattle is a young city that hugs an island-filled sound, where for over ten thousand years the stories and songs of First People were shared in longhouses and among cedars, huckleberries, and salal. While most of these stories are lost to history, there are notable exceptions; Vi Hilbert, a member of the Upper Skagit Tribe and the subject of Elissa Washuta's essay in this book, carried an entire language, Lushootseed, on her shoulders into the twentieth century. Washuta, a memoirist and member of the Cowlitz Indian Tribe, extends those traditions into the twenty-first.

With relatively little European immigrant history to claim, Seattle set its sights on the future, an attitude best expressed by the 1962 World's Fair, which gave us our iconic Space Needle. You know the highlight reel: planes, software, the web. Corporate office parks amid greenbelts. And yes, fine, okay, *coffee*. It's difficult to overstate the degree to which caffeine and the places we can consume it are responsible for Seattle's literary output. The literary effects of our recently legalized cannabis remain to be seen. I have a hunch we're in for a science-fiction boom.

Writers, already predisposed to solitude, can easily hide out here. If you're the kind of writer who wants to keep a low profile, the Pacific Northwest offers plenty of cloud cover. Pulitzer Prize–winning playwright August Wilson, whose legacy rests on a cycle of plays set in Pittsburgh, Pennsylvania, lived in Seattle, unbeknownst to many, as did, for a time, Thomas Pynchon, whose early career included a stint as a technical writer for Boeing (a great place to learn about rocket science).

The surrounding region's mountains and waterways, some of which are under an hour's journey outside the city, offer quiet places where a poet or novelist can hole up in a cabin and crank out pages. Children's author and illustrator Doris Burn, whose books *The Summerfolk* and *Andrew Henry's Meadow* capture the late afternoon shadows of the San Juan Islands in pen and ink, produced most of her work on Waldron Island, a speck in the

Salish Sea that boasts no electricity or running water. When I met her in 2007 at her home on Guemes Island, she told me how she'd written and illustrated her books by kerosene lantern and taken a train from Seattle to New York in search of a publisher, an extreme example of the lengths Northwest writers have gone to get their work into the world.

For many writers who call Seattle home, getting their work published means taking 7 a.m. phone calls from Manhattan, or making sure to send an e-mail by 2 p.m., before an editor's train departs to Brooklyn. Chad Harbach, in his provocative anthology *MFA vs NYC*, identifies two loci for America's literary culture— one in Manhattan, the other spread archipelago-like among the country's Master of Fine Arts creative writing programs. It's a useful way to conceptualize American literary culture, but it's becoming clear to many of us that the concept is incomplete. It's not just MFA vs. NYC. It's MFA vs. NYC vs. SEA.

Which brings me to Amazon. Pivoting off what Nick O'Connell said, I'd argue that the chapter of American literature we're currently witnessing is the story of how poorly Manhattan editors understand an e-commerce company from Seattle. As I write this in the spring of 2015, the controversial retailer has been in the news a lot, most notably for its contentious negotiations with one of the Big Five publishers, but also for international labor and tax matters, whose complexity warrants more pages than I'm prepared to produce. No one can deny Amazon's impact on the publishing industry, and the nature of that impact is a subject that deserves its own book. But this isn't that book.

The writers in this anthology are intimate and knowledgeable about Amazon in ways that few American authors can be. If they haven't worked there themselves, they no doubt have close friends or family members who have. I, for one, worked there twice, first from 1998 to 2000 as a customer service rep, when the company grew from just selling books to other product categories, then as an editor on the Media Merchandising team from 2004 to 2007. Let's just say that, like many writers in Seattle, my relationship with Amazon is as complicated as a lovers' quarrel.

I will say this about Amazon—it has brought international attention to Seattle in ways that are debatable but undeniable. These days, writers in Seattle aren't wondering how to get a book contract in New York; they're thinking about how to connect with readers in all corners of the globe. In June of 2013 at the Elliott Bay Book Company's fortieth-anniversary reading, I proposed that Seattle follow the example of our sister city Reykjavík, Iceland, and make a bid to join UNESCO's Creative Cities network as a City of Literature. This international program was established to recognize various cities' contributions to artistic expression and to encourage the economic development of creative industries through cultural tourism and artistic collaboration.

The overwhelmingly positive response to my suggestion at Elliott Bay knocked me back on my heels. I came to understand how hungry Seattle's books community is to forge alliances with cities that represent some of the world's great literary traditions. As of this writing, the nonprofit organization Seattle City of Literature is preparing a bid to join this network, and by the time you read these words, we may know whether we were successful.

Regardless, readers and writers in our future-facing city welcome the expressions of the world's literary artists, some of whom write under conditions far less tolerant of dissent or of themes related to sexuality, politics, or cultural identity than we experience. Drag your finger along the spines of the fiction section at Elliott Bay or Third Place Books, and browse the poetry-only shop Open Books, and you'll find a gratifying number of works in translation. We like to claim that a writer writing in any language in the world can find a reader in Seattle. And we're eager to engage readers far beyond our borders. If Seattle is to be recognized for its own contributions to literature, it must first be recognized as a city whose readers honor the world's literary traditions.

This collection of personal reflections by Seattle writers isn't meant to be comprehensive; the table of contents of this anthology could just as easily have been comprised of an entirely different list of writers. Rather, it's meant to give readers a taste of what it's like to hang out with a sampling of the novelists, poets, memoirists, and essayists who call Seattle their home. Here you'll find tales of classroom epiphanies, readings gone bad, and a surprising number of people walking through plate-glass windows or dressing up as Gertrude Stein. I also reached out to people who work in various corners of Seattle's literary economy—bookstore clerks, publishers, folks who run festivals and readings—and asked for their insights. Their profiles are distributed among the essays.

As these writers' reflections started arriving in my in-box, I noticed two things. One, this truly is a writing *community*. Little did they know, these writers were cross-referencing and name-checking each other in way I hadn't anticipated. Two, this community is bound by a sense of responsibility for one another. It's through various gigs, jobs, workshops, and bookstore experiences that friendships among writers grow. It's through these friendships that their work gets better.

Thanks for reading. Let's get on with our show.

Ryan Boudinot
Capitol Hill
May 2015

PART 1

REMEMBERING

ELISSA WASHUTA

ON VI HILBERT

I did not know about Vi Hilbert and her incredible work when I arrived in Seattle in 2007, but I knew that I was stepping into a place where the oral tradition pulses in every arm of our literary world. We cannot work with words here without working them aloud, whether at microphones or in small circles.

This unbroken oral storytelling tradition has existed in the Puget Sound area for more than ten thousand years. What we know now as Seattle has long been a gathering place; the Lushootseed name of the precolonial village at the site of the current city translates to "little crossing-over place." Before the arrival of European settlers, the Coast Salish people told stories solely in Lushootseed, Whulshootseed, and other Native languages of the region; now, these stories continue to have an important place in holding the world together, and English and other languages have entered the Coast Salish world along with the visitors who brought them.

The mingling of literatures and traditions from the various peoples who now live here represents a recent development in the region's long history of building enduring structures using words. I see Seattle as the crossing-over place it has been for so long, a village perfectly situated for writers to converge and exchange ideas.

The way of life for this area's Native peoples were significantly impacted by the arrival of Europeans in 1792, but Coast Salish peoples continue to thrive, initiating cultural and linguistic revitalization and continuation efforts while maintaining tribal governments and, in many cases, reservations. Some, but not all, tribal peoples call these reservations home, and there is a significant urban Indian population in Seattle. Citizens of many Native nations now call this city home.

For thousands of years, Puget Salish peoples have maintained stories about the world's origin. Many stories concern a figure known as the Transformer, or the Changer, who changed animals, landscape features, and people into their current forms, and in doing so, brought balance to the world. They also tell of spirits known to be dwelling throughout the world, and they carefully maintain relationships with spirit powers through ceremony, as their help is necessary for personal and communal well-being.

The original language of the greater Puget Lowland area is Lushootseed, and its southern dialect, Whulshootseed, is spoken in many areas. Compared to English, Lushootseed features many more consonants and fewer vowels, requiring speakers to produce sounds at the back or sides of the mouth and creating multiple pronunciations for basic words. Present-day Lushootseed language conservation and education efforts have benefited from the lifelong work of Vi Hilbert, also known by the Lushootseed name taqʷšəblu, a member of the Upper Skagit Tribe.

Hilbert spent years transcribing and translating tape recordings of Lushootseed speakers, created by high-school music teacher Leon Metcalf in the early '50s. In order to create complete transcriptions, Hilbert sought out fluent speakers of Lushootseed who could help fill in gaps in her understanding. According to linguist Thom Hess, with whom Hilbert worked to locate Lushootseed-speaking elders, "No one else could have done this work, and almost no one would have been willing to. Thanks to her Herculean efforts, much more history, grammar, lexicon, and myth has been saved from oblivion than posterity had any right to expect." Of her work, Hilbert said, "[It was] work that the Creator was wrapping around me. I was ordained to do this work. It was always there, waiting for me to do." Continuing her work of transcription and translation, Hilbert moved on to other recordings, some of which were created in the early 1900s. Her archive exists at several locations, including the University of Washington, consistent with her desire to increase the availability of the material.

Hilbert also made her work available to the public through several books, published by the University of Washington Press, including *Haboo: Native American Stories from Puget Sound* and *Lushootseed Dictionary*. She then established her own publishing company, Lushootseed Press, and a nonprofit called Lushootseed Research, to increase public access to bilingual Lushootseed-English materials. She taught Lushootseed classes for fifteen years at the University of Washington and for two years at The Evergreen State College. Hilbert was named a Washington State Living Treasure in 1989 and received a National Heritage Fellowship from the National Endowment for the Arts in 1994. She passed away in 2008.

Thanks to her efforts, Lushootseed language education efforts are still flourishing throughout Puget Sound. Classes are offered at Northwest Indian College in Bellingham, in the Tulalip Tribes schools, and elsewhere. In addition, Lushootseed Research holds the Lushootseed Language Conference annually. And in Auburn, the Muckleshoot Tribal School offers education in Whulshootseed.

Vi Hilbert strove to pass on stories in Lushootseed and in English to any student who approached with a willingness to learn and to tend the stories as living beings. I think the greatness of Seattle's spoken-word poets, physically present writers like Sherman Alexie, and others who bring magic to the stage is possible because Native storytellers prepared the air for so many generations.

TOM ROBBINS

ON HIS FIRST READING, PLATE GLASS, AND MORE

If there was anything resembling a genuine "literary scene" in Seattle in the '60s and '70s, I suppose it would have occurred in faculty housing at the University of Washington, with Theodore Roethke and David Wagoner as its nucleus. The nearby Blue Moon was frequented more by leftist radicals and painters (such as Richard Gilkey, Lubin Petric, and Bill Cumming), but there were a couple of poets (John Pym and Pete Winslow) among the regulars, and a guy named Jack Leahy wrote an entire novel (later published) in a back booth there. The writer and legendary bigger-than-life bohemian figure Darrell Bob Houston would periodically erupt in flamboyant rants, but the nearest thing to an actual ongoing literary event at the Moon was this: A UW professor at the time (named Goldberg, Goldstein, Goldman, or something similar) was one of the world's foremost experts on Chaucer. He was also a boozer and denizen of the Moon, where graduate students would cram into his booth and buy him beer after beer to loosen his tongue so they might pick his brain about all things Chaucerian. Some of us would try to eavesdrop, but it was ultimately futile, because after the third or fourth round of schooners, all the conversation would be in Middle English.

One night at the Moon, Pym—a pretty good although undisciplined poet—stripped naked and walked through the plate-glass door—crashed right through the glass—and was last seen casually strolling east on Forty-Fifth Street, leaving a little trail of blood. Houston also occasionally disrobed.

In those days, my friends and I bought books (when we could afford them) exclusively at the University Book Store. More conventional Seattleites purchased their tomes at Frederick & Nelson. I don't recall any other options. Later, of course, I shopped at Elliott Bay.

As I've said elsewhere, drizzle drip for drizzle drip, salmon whisker for salmon whisker, no author has evoked this spectacularly mildewed corner of the US linoleum more eloquently and accurately than Ken Kesey in *Sometimes a Great Notion*, although if one wants a factual history of Seattle, the book to read is Murray Morgan's *Skid Road*. Recently Jim Lynch's *Truth Like the Sun* brilliantly evokes a particular period (around the time of the World's Fair) of Seattle's past.

You are probably aware that Thomas Pynchon lived in Seattle while working as a tech writer at Boeing. It's believed that he wrote at least some of *V.* while here. Years ago, I met a jazz musician who'd been Pynchon's Seattle buddy, and he showed me a photograph of the two of them. Having seen that photo, I realize why Pynchon never published his picture on one of his book jackets.

When it comes to potential amorous responses from female readers, it wouldn't have done him a bit of good. (Unlike my picture on the back of the hardcover edition of *Jitterbug Perfume*: holy moly!)

For *Another Roadside Attraction*, I was offered one and only one author event: a reading/signing at a smallish bookstore at Fourth and Pine, an area then favored by Seattle's streetwalkers and their potential johns. Only a handful of people showed up for the event, but one of them was Darrell Bob Houston, who, embarrassed for me, went outside and invited some of the prostitutes, to inflate the crowd. After a while, pimps came inside looking to see where their girls had gone, and since there were several jugs of red wine and maybe a reefer or two, there soon was a raging (and largely illiterate) book party. The store had a very nice beige carpet upon which was spilled a quantity of red wine. It was the last author event that store ever staged.

ERIC REYNOLDS

Associate Publisher, Fantagraphics

THE COMICS REVOLUTION DURING THE GRUNGE YEARS

The early '90s were not only heady days for people in the music biz. It bubbled over into all facets of local pop culture, not the least being the comics scene. Sub Pop was an early adopter in recognizing what Fantagraphics and its cartoonists brought to the city; we were still relatively unknown locally, sitting on the fringes of Seattle culture. There was no fanfare or keys to the city handed out when Fantagraphics moved from Los Angeles to Seattle, that's for sure. So having artwork by Charles Burns, Daniel Clowes, Jim Woodring, Peter Bagge, et al, all over Sub Pop's records and branding was definitely beneficial to us, and lent a certain legitimacy or street cred locally. We definitely rode Sub Pop's coattails a bit. We probably still do, to some degree.

TAKING A SEAT AT THE TABLE

Local graphic designers were among the first to really perceive and exploit what Fantagraphics brought to the table; there was a kinship between the cartoonists and illustrators we were publishing and designers like Jeff Kleinsmith and Hank Trotter at Sub Pop, Dale Yarger at the *Rocket*, Art Chantry, etc. I think most people still viewed artists like Clowes and Woodring as illustrators more than storytellers or literary figures. So they were being taken seriously on one level, yet not completely. But more so than they were in Los Angeles, which is just a tougher town, any way you slice it. It just took a bit longer for the Seattle literary community to embrace the idea that comics deserved a seat at the table. The idea of, say, having Peter Bagge do a book signing at Elliott Bay, or hearing Nancy Pearl talk about a graphic novel, would have still been kind of ludicrous.

THE QUINTESSENTIAL NORTHWEST GRAPHIC NOVEL

Someone recently asked me if I had a favorite quintessentially Seattle movie. The best thing I could come up with was Elvis's *It Happened at the World's Fair.* Yet it's easy to think of any number of quintessentially Seattle novels or graphic novels, which speaks to the literary scene, I think. One of my favorite graphic novels is Charles Burns's *Black Hole.* Burns is a graduate of Roosevelt High, and the park that much of the book is set in is Ravenna Park, not too far from our office, just down Roosevelt Way.

A BUNCH OF CARTOONISTS PLAYING VOLLEYBALL

Beginning in the mid-'90s, there was a group of cartoonists organized by Jim and Mary Woodring that would meet in Ravenna Park every Sunday and play volleyball. It was a who's who of the local comics community: the Woodrings, Ellen Forney, Rick Altergott, Ariel Bordeaux, Jim Blanchard, Pat Moriarity. Many others joined every week, including much of the Fantagraphics staff. I always thought it was funny that this group of comics nerd pals of Charles's was playing volleyball where he had set this horrific story about a group of teens afflicted by a deadly STD. Every time I'd see a University District street rat hanging in the park, I'd think he looked like a character out of *Black Hole.* At one point in the '90s, Coca-Cola licensed a bunch of Charles's art for branding its ill-fated OK Soda. There were billboards all around town that sported Charles's unmistakable heavy brushwork. So I'd be promoting *Black Hole* during the day, playing volleyball in the *Black Hole* park every Sunday, and seeing billboards of Charles's art back and forth during my daily commute. Life imitates art.

THE ONE BOOK BY A SEATTLEITE TO PUT IN THE HANDS OF A VISITOR

I would have to go with *Jim* or *The Frank Book*, both by resident genius Jim Woodring, and each containing a lifetime of wisdom and inspiration.

BEST NEIGHBORHOOD TO SET A MURDER MYSTERY

I'll go with Ballard, my hometown of the past twenty-plus years. I'm sure there are lots of buried secrets among the old Scandinavians on the fishing docks that the statute of limitations hasn't expired on yet.

BEST NEIGHBORHOOD TO SET A SCIENCE-FICTION NOVEL

Queen Anne. The Space Needle should figure prominently.

JONATHAN EVISON

ON ROCK MUSIC AND
(HIS OWN) BAD POETRY

I'll always remember the early '80s as being the heyday of Seattle, culturally. The Northwest was still isolated to some degree. Rents were affordable. Music and art developed organically. And unlike a lot of art and music scenes I've observed, everybody seemed to get along. But the early '90s were cool too. I watched many of my friends and old bandmates blow up into rock stars. It was an exciting time for them. Me, I was just slopping spaghetti and writing unpublished novels and listening to Sinatra. Everybody else had a guitar, a band, a developmental deal. I had a couple hundred form rejections and a chip on my shoulder. I was really active in the punk scene in the '80s, and later the rock scene, but it seemed like I was always the only writer. And my rock friends, they always believed in me, contrary to the body of evidence. They made me feel special because I wasn't playing a guitar.

Now, Seattle has an amazing literary community. We have the best indie bookstores in the country. We have the Seattle7, who, by the way, need to check their math, because there's like eighty of them. But that's what I'm saying—this place is rich with literary culture. I'm thrilled to be a small piece in the puzzle.

I could never abide bad poetry. Back in the early '90s, I used to host a night of intentionally bad poetry at this little tavern under the monorail on Fifth Avenue called the Ditto, owned by a dude named Pauletti, who looked like Rick Rubin. It was a terrible bar—nobody ever went there—which made it the perfect venue for my purposes. We would pack the place every week, which meant there were maybe twenty-five people. The poetry was hilarious. Mine was often considered the best—that is, the worst. People were belly-laughing at my stuff. *"O' the more I search, size, hypothesize, the farther lost I get in the muss-muddle fog of adolescentdom"*—that kind of thing. What I never told anybody was that those ham-fisted poems I was reading were written in earnest only a few years earlier. Seriously, you can't fake something that bad.

DEB CALETTI

ON DAVID WAGONER AND THE LONG HAUL

I once saw the great poet David Wagoner get out of his old blue car in the Hugo House parking lot. This was a handful of years ago; I was somewhere between book five and six at the time, and I was there to read a story I'd written for the first-ever evening of the Hugo Literary Series. When he first drove up, I didn't realize it was him. He was just a white-haired man maneuvering a car into a tight spot. I was probably worried about my paint job. But he parked just fine, and because I was early as always, I watched him move some papers around for a bit. He stuffed the papers into a valise (but I may be imagining the valise). And that's when I saw who it was.

This is not a story of a breathless fan glimpsing her hero. I'd already met and conversed with Mr. Wagoner several times, though I confess I mostly shied away from poetry after too many bad experiences with wombs and rotting apricots in verse. This may not even be a story at all, because nothing dramatic happened. He simply got out of the old car, wearing his usual sport coat and turtleneck. He edged sideways between our doors and scuffled off.

But I never forgot it, because something about the wise man and the old car and the papers made me think about a life spent as an artist. What it meant giving up and what it gave. I saw all his years right then, the two when he was nominated for the National Book Award, and all the ones before and after and in between, eighty-plus of them. I saw the commitment, and the toll this life takes. The shining moments. The way the toll is greater than the shining, but how the shining is still worth it.

By that point in my career, it was clear that there was no turning back for me, no becoming a banker or a librarian. By then, too, I knew something that aspiring writers often do not—that getting in the game is easy compared to staying in the game. I was already a little tired—a book a year, the constant feeling of wolves at your heels, the need to bring quality *every single time*, the criticism, criticism, criticism. So I watched Mr. Wagoner with something more than curiosity and even awe. I watched him as if he held some secrets. Secrets to the long haul.

Five or six more books followed for me, and now I know a bit more about those secrets, and why that moment had things to tell me. Here was the image: Mr. Wagoner, stepping out of his car in that Capitol Hill parking lot and walking into one of our city's literary organizations while carrying a sheaf of papers. And like a dream that flashes the cryptic pieces of the puzzle, here were the answers I could finally see. How do you stay in the game as a writer? How do you make this your life's work? With inspiration, for starters, and lots of it. The parking lot is in Seattle, because every day this city offers up the rich images you need. A seaplane splashes down, a bored but regal eagle gazes out from where he's perched on an evergreen bough. He seems deep in thought, and so are you, perhaps both contemplating your place in the food chain. A flock of crows commutes over your home every day at dawn and dusk. A moody cloud passes, ready to splat rain. The mossy Northwest settles into your work; it becomes a reappearing character, lovely on the exterior but harboring sharp-tongued private thoughts. The houseboats rock, and a bear lumbers down from the mountains, and another storm sends the garbage cans rolling down steep streets.

The working writer's life requires camaraderie and kinship too—it's impossibly lonely and difficult without them. Often, in the wider world of your fellow authors, you feel the hovering shadows of competition, the measuring of who has what, who might like to step on the back of your shoes. But you get out of your car and head to a writers' event *here*, in Seattle, because here it's all in the family. Sure, family still might measure and still might squabble, but blood is blood. Your friends are on your shelves. You whine and wine together, just you guys, at signings and fund-raisers and galas, at gatherings at the Liberty bar. Seattle's literary organizations helped raise you, as well, and the city's bookstores and libraries are now like the homes of relatives—the good kind of relatives who look out for you and make sure you bring home the leftovers. Through the years, these have become your people. You are a clan, with your own moat and your own feasts.

Of course, most important to the long haul, there is the daily work. That sheaf of papers. And papers. And papers. This is a private matter, an intimacy between you and the page that happens under your own roof. As any animal knows, though, the first trick of survival is finding a home that both shelters and feeds you. Mr. Wagoner turned on Eleventh Avenue and went up the Hugo House steps that day, and when he did, I felt a great deal of tenderness for him, and a great deal of respect. I felt gratitude, too, for the way a city makes an artist whole. I watched until I couldn't see him anymore. And then I picked up my own valise and followed him inside.

TREE SWENSON

ON CAROLYN KIZER

Carolyn Kizer wasn't someone who simply walked into a room—she made an entrance, altering the conversations and changing the electrical charge in the air the moment she appeared. She was impossibly glamorous, even when she arrived disheveled from a journey—as she did in 1984 when I first met her at the opening reception of a writers' conference. In the crowded room, people were stealing glances at the figure near the door and asking, "Who is that?"

Self-described in "So Big: An Essay on Size," Kizer noted, "I'm something over 5'10" in my bare feet, and I look . . . like a road-company Valkyrie." Though the woman who appeared at the reception looked nothing like the author photo of Kizer's much younger self that she'd recently sent Copper Canyon Press, I recognized the regal command and knew: it had to be Carolyn Kizer.

Carolyn created myths. Maybe that came from her time studying mythology with Joseph Campbell at Sarah Lawrence, or maybe it was just an innate sense of connection to the legendary. She was part of the first real school of poetry that sprang from the ground of this region, one of the "five poets of the Pacific Northwest" that Robin Skelton selected for his 1964 anthology of the same name (along with Richard Hugo, William Stafford, David Wagoner, and Kenneth O. Hanson).

Carolyn Kizer helped invent Seattle as a literary city. Though she grew up with cultured parents in Spokane—where she met thinkers and poets from an early age—and she lived for many years in other states, she is inextricably tied to this rainy city in the top left corner of the country.

While living here, Kizer was a student of Theodore Roethke at the University of Washington (after three children and a divorce from Seattle icon Stimson Bullitt—lawyer, broadcast executive, notable outdoorsman, and political activist). After learning from Roethke to take herself seriously as a poet, she cofounded and edited for seven years *Poetry Northwest*, a literary journal that was readily recognized as one of the best.

At a time when few women poets received much attention, Kizer was published by Doubleday. She reviewed books for the *New York Times Book Review*, the *Washington Post Book World*, and other publications. She was appointed the first director of literary programs at the National Endowment for the Arts. She was a force when women were rarely reckoned with.

I worked with Carolyn on four of her books published by Copper Canyon Press. The first, *Mermaids in the Basement*, came out the same year her book *Yin*, from BOA Editions, won the Pulitzer Prize. BOA's book won the Pulitzer, but Copper Canyon won the poet. Maybe she decided to stay with our press because she launched into poetry from the Seattle area, though she was long gone by then, or perhaps she relished the idea of having books come from a press with a female publisher.

Carolyn decided while working on her next book that I was her editor, despite the clear distinction agreed upon by me and my partner at the press, Sam Hamill, that he was the editor and I was the publisher and executive director of Copper Canyon. But famous feminist that she was, Carolyn insisted that I edit *The Nearness of You*, a collection of poems for men—friends, lovers, fellow poets, and her father—that she regarded as a companion volume to *Mermaids in the Basement*, subtitled *Poems for Women*. Outspoken always, Carolyn insisted not only on working with me, but acknowledging in the book that I was her "meticulous and devoted editor." She knew that I, like many other younger women, needed the encouragement she so readily gave—needed the push the same way she needed Roethke to push her to take herself seriously as a poet. Working with Carolyn was a turning point in my time at Copper Canyon Press.

As for the streak in Kizer that loved outrage, she preferred poets who had "a sting in the tail," such as Catullus and Juvenal. She was the queen of irony, with her wit and bite. She liked making her own rules and breaking others'. When she was signing broadsides for Seattle's great poetry bookstore Open Books, she sat in the office in back with the door closed, and, knowing beyond question that it was not allowed, she lit a cigarette. To remove any doubt that she didn't know better, she asked the broadside's publisher not to tell John and Christine, the ever-generous proprietors of the store.

In the essay "Western Space," Kizer recounts Richard Hugo's statement that what differentiated poets from other people was that "Poets think about death *all the time*." A poet of the West herself, she wrote, "There is something about our great spaces—of desert and plains and fields, and the vast skies overhead—that makes us feel small, and fragile, and mortal." She may have felt fragile, but she had an air of invincibility. She shared many traits that are common in Seattle: she was rugged, irreverent, venturesome, and obstinate, and held to her political convictions. Add to that her intelligence, wit, and generosity—particularly to her students and to women writers of all ages—and there you have the myth of herself that the poet Carolyn Kizer created.

KEVIN CRAFT

Editor, *Poetry Northwest*

HOW THE REGION'S OLDEST LITERARY MAGAZINE GOT STARTED

Poetry Northwest was founded in June 1959 by Carolyn Kizer, Richard Hugo, and Nelson Bentley, among others. Though it has passed through several iterations since its late '50s debut, the core mission has remained steadfast: to provide a prominent platform for regional, national, and international writers to intersect with an audience of rough, ready, and discerning readers.

We aim to represent our vital corner of the continent to a broader audience, to serve as the go-to gateway for emerging writers to connect with readers beyond their local guilds and neighborhoods, and to attract and sustain readers with the promise of discovery. We straddle two worlds, really—older readers deeply connected to the history of Northwest letters, and newer audiences looking for some perspective in all the gush and flux.

DON'T MAKE THE MISTAKE OF THINKING *POETRY NORTHWEST* ONLY PUBLISHES NORTHWEST POETRY

People sometimes think we publish only Northwest writers or themes, what Hugo called (in an epistolary poem to Kizer) "the primal source of poems: wind, sea / and rain, the market and the salmon." This is patently untrue, and has been since the beginning. Geography is less an orienting aesthetic, more a state of mind: edge writing, out here in the hinterlands of consciousness.

POETS AND ARTISTS GETTING UP IN EACH OTHER'S BUSINESS

Kizer was connected to the visual arts scene in midcentury Seattle and managed to convince Mark Tobey to paint an original image for the first cover (a detail of which remains our logo today). Morris Graves designed covers for early '60s issues too. Edward Gorey was another prominent contributor of illustrations. Kizer served as editor for seven years, giving the magazine a distinct voice—her voice, simultaneously warm, generous, and austere, classically restrained yet palpably excited to be breaking new ground—before leaving in 1966 to take up a position as the very first director of literary programs at the newly established National Endowment for the Arts.

THE DAVID WAGONER ERA

Beginning in the winter of 1963, *Poetry Northwest,* which started out independently, was adopted by the University of Washington. Kizer later handed the magazine off to David Wagoner, who served as editor for thirty-six years. Wagoner preserved the poetry-only format and quarterly publication schedule through five different decades, from 1966 to 2002—a remarkable feat—but eventually, changing times and financial difficulties closed in around the magazine, and the University of Washington withdrew its support in 2002.

BABYLONIAN EXILE

In August 2005, the University of Washington appointed David Biespiel the new editor of *Poetry Northwest,* with an agreement that the editorial offices of the magazine would relocate to the Attic Writers' Workshop (now the Attic Institute) in Portland, Oregon. The new series resumed publication in March 2006, in a larger, trade-magazine format, appearing biannually as a print edition, with new monthly features published online. Circulation quickly rebounded. I think of the time the magazine spent in Portland as a kind of benign Babylonian exile—a necessary step in the magazine's evolution—modernizing its perspective, broadening the roots of community support. It's one more thing that Seattle and Portland now share in common. I was appointed editor in January 2010, returning the editorial offices to the greater Seattle area.

POETS WHO GOT THEIR STARTS IN THE PAGES OF *POETRY NORTHWEST*

Those published first or early in their careers include James Wright, Beth Bentley, Joan Swift, Maxine Kumin, Robert Wrigley, Bob Hicok, May Swenson, and so many more. Some of John Berryman's "Dream Songs" first appeared in the winter 1962–63 issue. Hayden Carruth, William Stafford, Patricia Goedicke . . . the tables of contents of *Poetry Northwest* form a who's who of American letters.

KIZER AND HUGO

When the magazine first published former editor Richard Hugo in winter 1961, Kizer wrote, for his contributor bio,

> Richard F. Hugo is an ex-editor of this magazine, an association which was a source of satisfaction to us all. His brand-new book, *A Run of Jacks* [Hugo's first], has been published, also with tender loving care, by the University of Minnesota Press, and is dedicated to Kenneth Hanson. We apologize for being so lyrical about poets, publishers, and each other, in these notes,

and will try not to let it happen again. It's just that there have
been all of these *splendid* books.

You can hear in these lines, characteristic of Kizer, that warmth and
generosity I mentioned earlier—the sense of community endeavor, of
sharing in each other's successes, which I think has always been typical
of literary life in Seattle, out here on the fast frontier.

THE ONE BOOK BY A SEATTLEITE TO PUT
IN THE HANDS OF A VISITOR

I'll stick to my guns here and suggest *The Collected Poems of
Theodore Roethke*, because it contains the seeds of all that's dis-
tinctive in the poetry that has emanated from this city for the last
sixty-plus years. Without Roethke, Seattle's midcentury vibrancy as
a literary town would have been far more dissolute, if it existed at all,
both in poetry and all that poetry underwrites in a literary ecology. His
classes were the focus of that first and second generation of writers
we still celebrate today: Hugo, Kizer, Wright, Wagoner, etc. He put the
Blue Moon (that seminal literary dive in the U District) on the map.
This is well-known. Less visible, perhaps, is his lingering influence on
subsequent generations. He brings that quirky sincerity, that nursery
rhythm edging into darkness, the firsthand struggle on the frontier of
self-reckoning, the deep love of etymology, rhythm, and rhyme that
many of our contemporary poets—from Richard Kenney and Heather
McHugh to Rebecca Hoogs and Kary Wayson—still use so inventively.
His *Collected Poems* is as much a primer on the territory as any field
guide to flora and fauna of the Pacific Northwest.

NEIGHBORHOOD BOOKSTORE OF CHOICE

Phinney Books, on Greenwood and Seventy-Fourth. I live in Greenwood, and we've had some good bookstores, mostly used books—such as the thriving Couth Buzzard Bookstore—but many of them have closed in recent years. So it's doubly special that Phinney Books is here, and doing well. It took over the space and niche that Santoro's Books occupied: a thoughtfully curated list of fiction and nonfiction, with ample sections devoted to kids' books, YA fiction, and, yes, even poetry. It's owned and managed by Tom Nissley, the most literate of our local *Jeopardy!* champs. He can size you up with a few questions and recommend a book you didn't know you needed to read. Last book I bought there was for my daughter: *Wonder* by R. J. Palacio. That, and an amazing cookbook by Becky Selengut called *Shroom*. If not exactly like mushrooms, it's good to see independent bookstores flourishing again to a certain degree. The landscape would be much less savory without them.

ED SKOOG

ON PETER BAGGE, OPEN BOOKS,
THOM JONES, AND *LITRAG*

The great Seattle cartoonist Peter Bagge bears some responsibility for my moving to town in the mid-'90s. In college in Kansas,
I loved Bagge's comic *Hate*, starring Buddy Bradley, set in the
beau monde of grungy slacker loserdom of early-'90s Capitol Hill.
Bagge's Seattle presented a slightly functioning society of the kind
of fools I wanted to be around, rather than the high-achieving farm
kids who populated my Kansas ag college. Many of my friends felt
the same, and we moved to Seattle in droves after graduation, and
most of us have stayed. Not all of my Kansas group are writers, but
we're all readers. We meet on Wednesday evenings for spaghetti at
the Tin Hat in Ballard, not far from where Peter Bagge lives. When
I met him recently, and informed him of his culpability, he hung
his head and said he got that a lot but we all had misread him, of
course. And it's true: as the title implies, *Hate* is kinda negative and
satirical and wiseassed—a *critique*. I prefer my misreading, letting
Hate remain as one mumpsimus of many that organizes my obstinate adult choices.

Christine Deavel and John Marshall opened their poetry bookstore in Wallingford, Open Books, about the time I moved to town. My first visit destroyed me. Confronted by their comprehensive inventory, I realized how little I knew about poetry, and that I might as well just wrap a cutthroat trout in my MFA diploma. (Was there an actual diploma?) So with their assistance, I finally got down to work. The first books I purchased from them were the collected poems of W. H. Auden and the collected poems of Joseph Brodsky. I've since bought about two hundred books from them over the years, none of them trifles. Open Books is like a hardware store run by engineers. Despite its calm, reasonable design, the simple white walls, the books in their places, one bench in the middle, and the thoughtful lightning, despite all of this, it's a tough room, politely rigorous, modestly cavernous, pleasantly infinite. It's a weight room.

Sometime in the late '90s, the great short-story writer Thom Jones read in the basement of the Elliott Bay Book Company down in Pioneer Square. It's my understanding that Jones, who lived in Olympia, has been sidelined since about that time with epilepsy, diabetes, and other conditions stemming from his time as a boxer. He worked a janitor at a high school while writing the stories in *The Pugilist at Rest*, which are great and chilling stories that I'd put up against anybody else's work in any language or time. I don't remember what he read, but I remember his body and his voice, at once both incredibly strong and incredibly frail. Here was a suffering hero out of Homer's battlefields, or Homer himself, battled down in frame and imagination, yet still with a lethal power. Despite that, he was also hilarious. His daughter and her friends were in the crowd. He was an enormous force. It was really something.

The power of the reading stemmed from a local kind of mystery. He was unapproachable, reluctant, brooding. He embodied some of the old Pacific Northwest force, the darkness of old-growth forests and the brutality of their felling, the way body and mind can be mangled in the distant outposts. That part of the Pacific Northwest which is an extension of Siberia is in his writing, and perhaps because I didn't understand the full, intense humanity of his stories prior to the reading, it really walloped me down there in the basement of the old Elliott Bay, underground in the old city.

I led writing workshops at a youth shelter for several years, facilitated by Hugo House. Every Tuesday, I'd fill a few hours between the end of school and the beginning of dinner at a couple of pushed-together tables, writing poems and stories, or just talking, with a few kids emerging from rough places. You don't end up homeless at sixteen because you're boring. A lot of the kids identified as writers, artists, or musicians, and not merely aspirationally: they had stories to tell, metaphors to explore, images to articulate. A lot of it was painful, but a lot of it wasn't, and I learned more about the ways that personal development is intertwined with the development of the imagination. We could see Mount Rainier from the shelter's porch. But I don't think we ever got around to writing about it.

After graduate school in Montana, in 1996, I intended to move to Prague with my poetry blood brother A. J. Rathbun, but as the summer after grad school went by and we still hadn't looked into tickets, our European escape plan faltered. I was trying to write a novel in Abilene, Kansas; A. J. was writing poems and hanging out in Chicago. We were too late for Prague, anyway, I've been told. A. J. came out to Seattle a few months after I got here, and stayed on my couch for a spell, then went to work for one company after another, and has now long been a hardworking Seattleite (with some time off in Italy for good behavior) and an author of books of poetry and the good life, up in Loyal Heights. But from some hazy time in the late '90s until 2007, A. J. and a friend, Derrick Hachey, ran a literary magazine called *LitRag* out of their houses. *LitRag* was totally boss, with silk-screened covers, local and far-flung contributors, and the best parties in town when each issue was released. Many of the contributors have since been converted into tech professionals, who no longer write much. Perhaps they will again. These little magazines, with their mayfly lives, are critically important to the literary habitat, but they disappear, without a sound usually, get paved over, and no one notices. Each issue is a victory and brings something forward, though I'm still not sure what the destination is.

KATHLEEN ALCALÁ

ON TESS GALLAGHER

The first time I saw Tess Gallagher, she was wearing a pith helmet. I was not sure why—perhaps she had just arrived from a costume party. I didn't think too much of it, because my father used to wear one now and then. Maybe they were especially comfortable in hot weather. It turned out that, in Merry Prankster fashion, she had an entire wardrobe of exotic headwear.

The next time I met her, she was with Ray Carver, and he was dying. He gave a last reading at the University of Washington and answered a few questions from the audience. He was a shy man, uncomfortable in front of a crowd. Still, the students were in awe of him. What sort of person could write a story as good as "Cathedral"? Ray put everything he had into his writing, and the next thing we knew, at the age of fifty, he was gone.

They made a nice couple: Ray with his heavy, serious brow, Tess with her open, luminous face. They were both from working-class backgrounds, kissed by that mysterious muse that comes to fetch poor children in spite of and because of the emotional silences around them. As a teen, Tess made her way from her home in Port Angeles to Theodore Roethke's last workshop.

I don't think it was until the third time I met Tess that I noted her way of speech. She pronounced everything very clearly, almost too clearly, as though she was sure we were all hard of hearing. Tess has a lot to say, it turns out, and doesn't want to repeat herself.

Tess means everything that she says, and is not shy with her opinions. I have heard her give several craft lectures over the years, and she is brilliant. Other writers who make their livings by teaching or giving the occasional speech have formulated at least portions of their talks over years of practice. If Tess does this, it is hard to tell. Each speech seems fresh, as if she had just discovered the point earlier that day and was completely convinced that it would change the way she wrote, and should change the way you write too.

Others have remarked on her mode of speech, and think perhaps she has a bit of an Irish accent. It's possible, she says. Her ancestors came from Ireland, where they were probably fishermen. Tess will throw a line in the water if given a chance as well.

In his last years, after an unhappy first marriage, Ray found happiness with Tess. They would both write all day, he scribbling notes to himself and Tess, and leaving them scattered around her Sky House in Port Angeles.

Tess and Ray used to go into Seattle to visit painters Alfredo Arreguin and Susie Lytle, Arreguin's wife. Both Tess and Ray made their way into Arreguin's intricate canvases. Those conversations should have been recorded, saved somehow for the rest of us.

Out of them came the story "Menudo," initially part of the movie made of Carver's stories, *Short Cuts*, by Robert Altman.

"When you at last begin to seize those things / which don't exist," Tess writes in "One Kiss," "how much longer will the night need to be?"

She drives over to Whidbey Island now and then to give a talk at the Northwest Institute of Literary Arts. Once, she arrived with a cast on her foot. Another time, with a small dog. Or was that at the same time, the cast and the dog? She's always cheerful, always patient and generous with students and faculty alike, even when their only question is, "What was he like?"

ROBERT SINDELAR
Managing Partner, Third Place Books

MEMORABLE VISITORS

Ann Patchett. You'll see why if you watch the video of her dramatic recitation of the Saint Crispin's Day speech from *Henry V* at BookExpo in 2012—she brought tears to many an eye. Another amazing experience was seeing eight hundred tweens giddy with excitement and waiting over an hour to hear John Green. Anyone who is remotely cynical about youth and the future of reading would be instantly cured by witnessing this. At one point a fourteen-year-old boy leapt on the stage with a ukulele and taught the entire crowd a song, which everyone sang while waiting for the event to start.

**MOMENT IN WHICH SEATTLE'S CULTURE
  CLASHED WITH A VISITING AUTHOR'S**

Martin Amis visiting Seattle in the mid-'90s (for *The Information*), when I worked at Elliott Bay. His reading is done and he's signing books, but he needs to smoke. There's no smoking in the Elliott Bay Café, but it's Martin Amis, so they let him. So he's got a cigarette lit, someone's brought him an ashtray, and he's signing away for the long line of fans. About halfway through the line, a customer says to him, "Mr. Amis, I love your work, and I really get all the dark stuff you write about, but I have to tell you, those things will kill you." Amis looks up from the book he's signing, grins a bit (which is quite a lot for

Martin Amis), and says, "Well, I know that—it says it right there on the pack, doesn't it?"

WHO KNEW SHE'D BECOME SUCH A FAMOUS SHOPLIFTER?

In the '90s, there was a really busy Saturday at Elliott Bay, and the store was packed. We had a line at the front counter, and the alarm went off by the front door as a couple people were leaving. I was closest, so it was my job to stop them and see if they had taken anything. When I looked over, I saw a girl with a baseball cap on and a guy with kind of long hair. They were slowing down but not really stopping. I called out to them, "Excuse me, could you just—?" And as they turned to me, I saw that it was Winona Ryder, with Dave Pirner from Soul Asylum. I had that weird moment of "Oh, it's you" and immediately felt really awkward and nervous, and so I just waved them along saying, "Oh, it's all right, never mind." Because they were famous, right? Why would they steal something? A few years later, I was watching the news, and there was this huge story about Winona Rider getting convicted for shoplifting. I still can't believe I let them go.

SEATTLE WRITER WHOSE NEXT BOOK WE
SHOULD ALL LOOK FORWARD TO

Karl Marlantes. Before I read his debut novel, *Matterhorn*, my thought was, *Do I really need a six-hundred-page book about Vietnam in my life right now?* Twenty pages in, I realized I did. It was so unexpected. No matter how many books or films you have experienced about the Vietnam War, everyone finds something completely new in *Matterhorn*. I can't wait to see what he does next.

BEST WAY TO KICK OUT AN UNRULY CUSTOMER

If they're violent, tell them you can't fight them in the store but you'd happily fight them out front. (Make sure someone has already called 911 and you have the keys to lock the door.) This has worked more than once.

THE ONE BOOK BY A SEATTLEITE TO PUT IN THE HANDS OF A VISITOR

If they want a book that gives the flavor of the area, I'd give them Jim Lynch's *The Highest Tide*. The scenes in that book around the tide pools couldn't take place anywhere else in the world.

BEST LITERARY PERFORMER

For all local authors, hands down it would have to be Sherman Alexie. That's less him reading his work than just the natural free-flowing riffing he does when talking about his work. For local authors reading their own work—Charles Johnson. Charles Johnson could make reading his grocery list interesting.

BEST NEIGHBORHOOD TO SET A MURDER MYSTERY

Someone must have already set a noir novel in and around the Seattle Underground. If not, they should. Cobblestone streets, dark, dank stairwells—it's perfect.

BEST NEIGHBORHOOD TO SET A SCIENCE-FICTION NOVEL

There's a good story in the idea that Fremont was created and founded by a group of aliens that crash-landed and began breeding in that area.

MOST RIDICULOUS QUESTION A CUSTOMER EVER ASKED

My first bookselling job, a customer comes in and says, "Do you have the book *Get Rich Overnight*?" I look it up and say, "Sorry, I don't, but I could have it for you in a few days." She says, without the slightest sense of irony, "No, I can't wait that long," and hurries out of the store.

BEST DAY JOB FOR A WRITER IN SEATTLE

Working in a bookstore. (I might be a bit biased.)

PART 2

LEARNING

MATT BRIGGS

ON DISCOVERING THE LITERATURE
IN HIS OWN BACKYARD

When I was eighteen, I lived in White Center and enrolled in a class at the ASUW Experimental College taught by two recent poetry MFA graduates from the University of Washington, Frances McCue and Bobby Anderson. The class took place in Padelford Hall, near the Collegiate Gothic humanities buildings on the campus's Quad, a grassy field bordered with cherry trees and lined with ancient red-brick paths. It had been protected by a student protest in the mid-'60s, when the administration was going to rip up the trees and pave the courtyard. The Quad had been untouched for so long that it was easy to imagine a time when Theodore Roethke was making his way across campus to a class dressed in his professional business suit, or making one of his famous maniacal entrances, such as climbing up the vines to enter through a window.

During one lecture, I made his student Tess Gallagher stutter when I heckled her about Roethke. "How can you think of

Theodore Roethke as a Pacific Northwest poet," I asked, "when he mostly writes about Michigan and is from Michigan?"

Gallagher repeated my blasphemy. "How can I think of him as a Northwest poet?" she said. "Why, he walked this very hall. He crossed the Quad. He climbed in through these very windows!" And that settled it for her. He was, for Gallagher, a Pacific Northwest poet because he had taught in the classrooms at the University of Washington.

Many of the English classes were taught in the tiny rooms of Padelford, and when we were kicked out of our assigned room, our small class of about eight student poets and two teachers would meet under a bulletin board on the second floor until we eventually found an empty room. It was winter. The campus was dark. The Quad was littered with brittle lichen-covered cherry tree branches. I would open one of the heavy old doors and find myself on the industrial linoleum, where I would meet the other students and we would hunt for a room.

Although Frances McCue had attended the graduate program at the UW, she was also involved in other, non-UW literary events around town. She ran a reading series with Matthew Stadler and Jan Wallace called the Rendezvous Reading Series, which was in the JewelBox Theater at the Rendezvous on Second Avenue, and one year she crashed the summer writers' conference at Centrum in Port Townsend. She seemed genuinely interested in her students. It wasn't merely enough that we wanted to write poems. She asked questions. She wanted to know *why* we were taking a poetry class. And it was clear that she was not a Seattleite. She talked a lot.

Bobby Anderson was a tall sandy-haired guy with acne scars. He wore a kind of old-fashioned leather jacket; it wasn't painted with the names of punk bands and was in pretty good shape. He worked in the circulation department at the *Seattle Weekly*. In 1990, the *Seattle Weekly* was a vibrant paper that published long articles by the likes of Fred Moody and David Brewster, comics by Lynda Barry, and occasional articles by writers like Jonathan Raban and Tom Robbins. I had read an article the previous Christmas by Raban about the "grey zones" of the city—that is, the neighborhoods where no one knows who lives there (except the people who live there). These are the neighborhoods people omit if you draw a map of the city, and living in a margin neighborhood between White Center and Burien, I felt like I was in a grey zone, that I was doomed to be a writer of the grey zones.

Bobby Anderson had actually grown up, he would reveal over the course of the class, near White Center, in the High Point projects at the top of Pigeon Point. He was a born and bred Seattleite. It was from McCue and Anderson that I first really learned about White Center poet Richard Hugo, who had worked at Boeing as a technical writer in the '50s and '60s, and had lived near West Marginal Way, less than a mile from my apartment. I read his first three books of poetry right away in his collected works, *Making Certain It Goes On*, and I read *The Triggering Town*, his short book of advice to poets and writers.

In those small, random rooms where we met, our class shared the poems we wrote, and we would get oblique assignments and work some more. I don't really write poetry anymore, and I never had aspirations to be a "poet" but felt, as a prose writer, that it paid to learn how to write poetry, since poets seemed so technically adept about how sentences and figurative language work. Prose writers tended to talk about what something was about, and if they believed it. Poets tended to talk about words, and if the words "worked." Hugo's book claimed, for instance, that all Northwest poets had to use the word "salal." He also discussed the different hues of "grey" vs. "gray." Most people see this as an Anglo vs. American spelling, but Hugo felt they carried different colors. That's how important words are to poets.

I saw an interview with Iggy Pop years later, and he talked about working on "owning" the sounds the Stooges made. They couldn't use a particular sound—the sleigh bell, maybe, in "I Wanna Be Your Dog"—until they owned it. It wasn't about a wide range of novel sounds, but rather mastering a limited range of simple sounds. And I felt in McCue's class, the stirring of my own awareness that this was how language could work. It wasn't about learning rare hundred-dollar words, but rather honestly owning the words you did use.

Part of this process for me was to have McCue and Anderson read my poems and not really connect with them. They didn't say, "Oh, these are bad." Instead, McCue regarded them as puzzles that she couldn't really figure out, like bundles of knotted string. I'm sure they were awful, but one of the pleasant things about our class was that it wasn't about evaluation but about figuring out what we were up to, even if we ourselves didn't know at that moment. Once, following five minutes of silence after I read a poem I'd xeroxed and brought to the session, McCue said to me, "It's like you have crammed a closet full of antique furniture." That was enough of a response for me. I took that home and stewed on it.

I had no way of knowing then that Frances McCue would go on to become one of the founders of Richard Hugo House. The writing center quickly found its voice when the first writer-in-residence, Rebecca Brown, began a reading series called the Sketch Club, which mixed up writers from the various circles of writers in Seattle. Unlike Red Sky, the UW's Castalia, or the Rendezvous Reading Series, concrete poets, nature poets, and fiction writers were all rolled up into Hugo House. The impulse to find common, unifying threads came to a head in 1998, in the circus of the Gertrude Stein-a-Thon, a twenty-four-hour reading and performance of Stein's work that was the inspiration of Brown and the poet Nico Vassilakis. My friend, the actor Skip Pipo, and I performed a sequence from Stein's writing advice book, *How to Write*, as two dueling Steins. I remember seeing great performances from *Paris France*, and Judith Roche reading *Lifting Belly*. Gertrude Stein and Hugo House provided the space and means for everyone to come together.

I once went to Brentano's bookstore in Westlake Center and asked a clerk there for a recommendation of contemporary short stories, and he recommended *Where I'm Calling From* by Raymond Carver. It was a hardcover book with the title set in Bernhard and an Edward Hopper painting of a suburban street on the front. In short, the graphic design of the Atlantic Monthly Press did not match the stories inside the book at all. Even the back dust jacket image of Raymond Carver wearing the kind of bomber jacket that was a fad for a couple of years after the movie *Top Gun* was released in 1986 didn't really evoke the stories in the book.

Carver's stories, in particular the stories in *Will You Please Be Quiet, Please?* and *What We Talk About When We Talk About Love*, were set in a kind of timeless place of poverty and Formica that I recognized from growing up. It made me realize I could write stories about what seemed mundane to me. Later, I found out he'd grown up in Yakima, the son of a saw filer who had been at the mercy of seasonal work. Carver himself worked marginal labor jobs, married young, and somehow managed to enter the university system during a period of explosive growth from the late '60s through the '80s. Carver drove bad cars, lived in crummy houses with unmowed lawns, and nearly drank himself to death. Despite there being a kind of cultural fascination with the terminal lifestyle of the end-of-the-line drunk in our culture, to me there was nothing romantic about it, or Carver's stories, and yet they were stylized in an oddly fascinating way that I couldn't put my finger on. In particular, the catchy way he repeated phrases throughout a story, and the way he used "he said," the refrain that is normally nearly invisible in a short story, as a kind of repeated sound.

Although Carver's stories were about a world I was familiar with and they were clearly written, they seemed somehow artless, and for me as a beginning writer that artlessness made me think, *Oh, I can do that!* And only when I tried to write a story in the style of "They're Not Your Husband" did I discover how difficult it was to make a story like that work.

Before I read Raymond Carver, I tended to write jumpy fantasy-style stories that had trouble making any sense at all. I'd written a story called "Leaves Shatter Like Skulls" and sent it to a local speculative-fiction magazine run by a writer who had been profiled in the *Seattle Post-Intelligencer*. She was one of those rare things in Seattle, a writer who made a living from her work, and she had been kind enough to send back a rejection letter that let me know she had read the entire story based on the evocative title. She went on to diagnose me with a personality disorder and recommended I see a psychologist as quickly as possible before someone came to harm. At eighteen, I regarded this exchange as an amazing step forward. Someone had read my work, even if it wasn't to her taste. She had actually considered it for publication, even if she'd found it wanting.

Raymond Carver gave me permission not to set my stories in colorful places, not to have fantastic events happen in my stories. They could be about the mundane world I was familiar with: White Center, the Duwamish Valley, Renton, and the Snoqualmie Valley.

Richard Hugo also pointed me to how the place I was familiar with could express itself in words, paragraphs, and sentences— with his first couple of books of poetry; his autobiography, *The Real West Marginal Way*; and even more, his book of writing advice, *The Triggering Town*. Hugo worked from the ground up, showing a particular interest in the names of things in his environment, from the rivers, the streets, and the neighborhoods to the people who lived there.

Frances McCue made much of Hugo's proclamation that all Northwest poets must use the word "salal." I think we had an assignment to include the word in a poem, just to get it out of our systems and be able to tell Richard Hugo we had done it. And yet, even ironically, there was a kind of permission in using "salal" or "Douglas fir," "devil's club," or "bleeding hearts"—to write what you know and not worry too much about explaining it.

Just the names of the poems in Hugo's first collection, *A Run of Jacks*, to me are evocative of particular places where I had been as a child: West Marginal Way, La Push, Alki Beach, and Snoqualmie. I had encountered the word "Snoqualmie" in a folk song quoted by Wallace Stegner in his collection of short stories, and I used to read that story just to see the name in print. Hugo has an entire poem about the Snoqualmie River, and in particular, the odd clay smell of the lower Snoqualmie.

The river starts high in the Cascades and winds a path to the Skykomish River forty-five miles away. The Middle Fork of the Snoqualmie passes through a green clay bank about two miles east of North Bend, and then after the confluence with its other two branches, when the river becomes immense, it drops off Snoqualmie Falls and meanders from Fall City to Monroe, across the dairy farms, and cornfields, and second-growth forest. Hugo wrote:

> To know it you recall crayola odors,
> first fields away from home

Hugo also wrote, "Assuming you can write clear English sentences, give up all worry about communication. If you want to communicate, use the telephone," and this advice was for me a revelation. Where Raymond Carver's stories demonstrated that the things that happen even to poor people are worth writing about and can make for great stories, Richard Hugo's poems showed that the obscure and peculiar turn of phrase, the local locution, the neighborhood name carry with them an essence of a place, just like the odor of the Snoqualmie carried with it the story of where the river had been.

Back in 1990, excited to learn of the presence of Richard Hugo in my general neighborhood, I went to the epicenter of the White Center literary world, the local branch of the King County Library System, a musty '70s-era brick structure with round portholes. It took me about an hour to walk there on a warm spring day. I found the poetry section, expecting it to be well stocked with the poetry of Richard Hugo. There was only a single volume, *White Center*. In contrast, there were about five copies of *Jimmy Stewart and His Poems*. But that didn't matter much to me. I was in a Raban grey zone in Hugo's White Center, considering the color of gray vs. grey.

RUTH DICKEY

Executive Director, Seattle Arts & Lectures

WHAT SEATTLE ARTS & LECTURES IS ALL ABOUT, IN A NUTSHELL

Seattle Arts & Lectures brings amazing writers and poets from around the world to Seattle, and we hire local amazing writers to work in year-long residencies in public schools to inspire kids to be the amazing writers of the future.

NUMBER OF CHILDREN AND ADULTS SAL REACHES EVERY YEAR

More than seventeen thousand.

NUMBER OF STUDENTS REACHED BY SAL'S WRITERS IN THE SCHOOLS PROGRAM

Over five thousand, across twenty-three public schools and at Seattle Children's hospital.

SEATTLE WRITER WHO DESERVES MORE ATTENTION

So many of them! I love Tom Nissley's *A Reader's Book of Days*. I adored Stephanie Kallos's *Broken for You*. And Garth Stein's new book is currently on my nightstand, next to Rebecca Hoogs's *Self-Storage*. I wish everyone also had these books on their nightstands! I have profound respect for *all* Seattle writers, and I love that the writing community is so supportive and generous.

BEST LITERARY PERFORMER

Gosh, I don't think I can give you the best answer, since I have only been back in Seattle for two years and there are so many local writers I haven't seen. With that caveat, I'd give this award to Daemond Arrindell. His poems are fantastic, and as a performer (whether performing his poems or speaking about why teaching writing to young people matters), he is absolutely inspiring.

BEST NEIGHBORHOOD TO SET A MURDER MYSTERY

I'd set the murder mystery in Pioneer Square on one of those foggy mornings when the tops of the buildings vanish.

BEST NEIGHBORHOOD TO SET A SCIENCE-FICTION NOVEL

I'd set the science-fiction novel in Fremont, centered around the Troll, which becomes a portal to another dimension.

NEIGHBORHOOD BOOKSTORE OF CHOICE

I absolutely adore bookstores, so I'll give you three:

- The bookstore I walk to most often is the Elliott Bay Book Company, where I recently bought *The Vacationers* by Emma Straub, a blank notebook, and more cards than one person could possibly need (because they are irresistible).

- The bookstore I drive to most often is Phinney Books, where I recently bought five books by Colm Tóibín and a Glittersweet bag, and ordered *Fire Shut Up in My Bones* by Charles M. Blow.

- The bookstore I drink coffee in most often is Queen Anne Book Company, where I recently got the new Haruki Murakami and *All the Light We Cannot See* by Anthony Doerr.

BEST DAY JOB FOR A WRITER IN SEATTLE

Teaching for Writers in the Schools.

KATHLEEN FLENNIKEN

ON FINDING HER COMMUNITY

There are many routes to becoming a writer, and I've taken a back one: less than young when I started, never to be a bright new discovery, full-on middle everything, married with children and a mortgage and an engineering degree thrown in. I love the Seattle writing community for welcoming and accepting me anyway. Our city of literature is a democratic and generous and open-minded city-inside-a-city, crisscrossed with routes leading in and around: I found my entrance at an ASUW Experimental College night class.

It was the early '90s, and I signed up for Introduction to Poetry Writing, taught by Michael G. Hickey: novelist-poet, dabbler in stand-up, charmer, cheerleader, future Poet Populist. The University of Washington campus lent our endeavor an air of respectability, but my fellow students looked unpromising. Microsofties. Retirement "crones." Twentysomething recent Seattle transplants. Many were wildly talented (and would go on to publication, prizes, and acclaim), but not one of us was legit. The obsession began—pen and recycled paper pulled from my purse—at jury duty, during preschool break, jotting lines at this series of traffic lights on Twenty-Fifth NE, over a pot of boiling pasta. Mike told me in the parking lot one night, "You're good," and I backed the car into a column, crushing the fender. I didn't even feel it.

I was thirty-two years old . . . thirty-five . . . forty. My husband and I added a third child. David Wagoner made me cry with his reading of "Their Bodies" in Kane Hall. I heard Galway Kinnell there, Seamus Heaney, Jorie Graham. But also, elsewhere, over the sounds of espresso machines: Molly Tenenbaum, Crysta Casey, Paul Hunter, Peter Pereira. I attended Esther Helfgott's It's About Time Writers Reading Series at the University Branch of the Seattle Public Library, where—if you signed up a year in advance—you could grab a fifteen-minute consultation. Catherine Wing invited me to be part of her Poor Man's MFA group. (This is before she got the real deal at the UW.) We all took turns assigning poets to read and discuss, and tentatively shared our own work in an atmosphere of solemnity and bashfulness. We were all falling in love. We were in love. I was almost ready to tell my friends. I told my friends. God, poetry is embarrassing.

Before I knew it, the city of Seattle—which always felt just a little too big, a little beyond the reach of my arms—had embraced me. I saw someone I knew at every poetry reading, no matter downtown or Ballard or Capitol Hill. At Open Books, I found the center of the poetry universe and learned I could take a few minutes with John and Christine. It's never mere gossip; it's poetry news briefs, poetry matchmaking, poetry decompression. And it's all so *normal*, as though it's perfectly *normal* to have an all-poetry bookstore in a medium-large American city with fewer than average churchgoers, that it's perfectly *normal* for poetry to be an actual physical destination—small, of course—that emits warmth and light.

I was bolstered along the way by organizations that hold up the literary community in Seattle—Artist Trust, King County's 4Culture, Seattle's CityArtist Projects program, Hugo House, the Seattle Poetry Festival (RIP), the Elliott Bay Book Company, University Book Store, and the Jack Straw Writers Program— which allowed me, eventually, to call myself a poet. Floating Bridge Press published me in the "Pontoon" section of its annual journal, and so I joined its Rolodex of poets. The *Seattle Review* and *Poetry Northwest* bestowed legitimacy, but also *Bellowing Ark*, the *Raven Chronicles*, the *Monarch Review*. Viva the little magazines.

One afternoon I found myself eating lunch with two MacArthur geniuses, Richard Kenney and Linda Bierds. Just the three of us, talking about poetry with a spectacular blue view of this beautiful city. *I don't belong here*, I remember thinking, but Rick and Linda were overlooking it, and I played along.

PETER MOUNTFORD

ON DAVID SHIELDS

When we showed up for David Shields's seminar in the spring of 2005, my cohort at the University of Washington's MFA program was feeling battered by six months of nonstop writing workshops. Most of us had moved to Seattle for the program—had arrived wide-eyed and eager, but since then our tender egos had been roughly handled in twice-weekly critiques. Like most creative writing MFA-ers, we worshipped at the altar of Raymond Carver, Lorrie Moore, Tobias Wolff, et al. On the first day of the seminar, Shields brushed all that aside, saying, "I don't want to be a dutiful craftsman, whittling away at this little gem of a short story. Husband and wife divorcing because—well, who cares? It hasn't changed in half a century, and feels embarrassingly antique to me."

My classmates and I were stunned.

For the next two hours, he went on like that. Soft-spoken, bespectacled, and bald, clad entirely in black, he was terrifyingly clear-eyed, casually calling upon countless quotations he'd committed to memory. His gaze lingered in the middle distance, at some point in the center of the long seminar table, as he dismantled—with unnerving precision—the entire premise of our work. At one point, he uttered the phrase "groaning contrivance," which became a fixture of my cohort's vernacular—you'd just scribble "GC" in the margin, and the author knew what you meant. Of course, we'd all worried hazily, quietly, about these exact questions, and then he just came out and said it—that he found most "serious" fiction incredibly dull. But it was clear, too, that his dismissal wasn't frivolous; he was desperate to read something that made him catch his breath.

Faulkner once said, "I rate us on the basis of our splendid failure to do the impossible." Those are the standards, and once you know them, you will never forget.

And while none of us followed fully in Shields's footsteps and none of us abandoned fiction, it's also true that none of us wrote the same again. I certainly didn't. Ever since, I've loved a good digression—most of my fiction is peppered with ruminative asides that read, frankly, a lot like essays. It's against the rules to write like that. In workshop, people will complain about it being abstract, about it being heady, about how you're telling and not showing. But at least they won't write "GC."

Years later, Shields and I wrote some screenplays together, and we even ended up flying down to Los Angeles to pitch a movie to the president of HBO. There, at the long table in the conference room at HBO's sleek headquarters, Shields stared off into the middle distance, setting up the story—laying the conceptual foundation—and when he was done, he leaned back, just like he used to do in class, and I knew it was my turn to take over.

CLAIRE DEDERER

ON DAVID WAGONER'S WORKSHOP

It was the summer of 1988. I was twenty-one. I had just dropped out of Oberlin College. Now I was back home in Seattle, not sure what would happen to me next. I thought I might be a writer. Actually, I was pretty sure of it, but I was all at sea as to how to begin, and a little afraid. I signed up for a couple of classes at the University of Washington, figuring it couldn't hurt. As it turned out, I loved the dreamy secret-clubhouse feel of summer school. You could do whatever you were doing in deadly earnest and yet tell yourself it wasn't really important.

My favorite class was a short-story workshop taught by the poet David Wagoner. A presence at once folksy and magisterial, Wagoner didn't like much of anything we short-story writers had to show him. We met a few times a week in a sunny, unromantic room in inglorious Loew Hall, and he explained to us that we were doing it all wrong. I found this bracing but a little intimidating. It seemed we had put in all the wrong things, and left out all the right ones. I didn't know it at the time, but I was being inducted into a rich tradition. Heaping abuse on students is a point of pride with hard-nosed, serious (and occasionally life-changing) writing teachers; I had simply never encountered this tradition before.

One hot morning in late July, Wagoner was especially frustrated with our work. Looking at us sternly from under his bushy white eyebrows, he scolded, "If you really want to improve, you must learn to copy other writers. Imitate the style of writers you love. Read them closely. Model your work on theirs. Rip them off."

Wasn't that, erm, cheating? I raised my hand. "Won't people know if we're ripping off other writers?"

He looked me in the eye, and what he said changed my writing life forever: "You are all such bad writers that no one will have any idea *what* you are trying to do." The class laughed nervously. Instead of feeling discouraged, I experienced a whoosh of excitement, like a wind through a door. I mentally ran through the Rolodex of the writers I loved at the time—Lorrie Moore, Calvin Trillin, Grace Paley, F. Scott Fitzgerald. I would attempt them all. I left Loew and walked purposefully to Suzzallo Library. I thought I might set myself up in a carrel and read a little and maybe even try to write. Protected by my very badness, I would make my assault on literature.

KATHLEEN ALCALÁ
ON CLARION WEST

So I will tell the real story. Samuel "Chip" Delany was reading from his work. He was my instructor that week at Clarion West, the science-fiction and fantasy "boot camp" to which I was committed for six weeks. I had recently completed an MA in creative writing at the University of Washington, but Clarion West offered a more immersive experience, with a strong emphasis on marketability. Although I began publishing my short stories in grad school, the business of writing did not receive much emphasis at the time. Clarion West—started by local writers Vonda McIntyre, J. T. Stewart, and Marilyn J. Holt—offered support for alternative writers and preparation for a "pro" career, one that would afford a decent living.

The reading was at the old Elliott Bay Book Company in Pioneer Square, the one with the dramatic staircase in the middle of the main room leading down to a café. At the back of the café was another room, its walls lined with odd old books. This venue for the author readings, which started with poet Colleen McElroy sometime in the '80s, was the site of my literary childhood and adolescence, where I came to hear and see "real writers" read from and talk about their books.

That evening started out just fine. It had been an unusually hot July, with no sign of the weather breaking. The audience was thoroughly engaged, many of them having read every book Delany—a novelist, philosopher, and brilliant futurist—had written. They were laughing in all the right places, or nodding knowingly. But at some point, the room just ran out of air. Things began to grow small, gauzy, as though I were witnessing everything through the wrong end of a telescope.

Hmm, I thought. Maybe only *I* had run out of air. Then I started seeing black spots in my line of vision. Since I was seated against the back wall, I figured I would be all right, cool. No one had to know I was blacking out.

The Clarion West students, who congregate every June and July to study with a series of six instructors, are a tough bunch. By maybe the fourth week, we were cranking out at least a story a week. One woman was cranking out a story a night, and the rest of us were trying to figure out how to disable her printer. We spent every day, all day, in a classroom at Seattle Central Community College, critiquing each other's work. At night, the out-of-towners stayed in hot little rooms in the dorms at Seattle University while the rest of us went home and continued to read and write. Fueled by Cheetos and candy bars, no one slept much.

Once, gazing out the window during class, a student said, "Look, a fire." We all had to stare hard for a moment to be sure it wasn't the product of our apocalyptic imaginations. Indeed, a bright blaze could be seen on a rooftop to the east.

Another student said, "That's my building," and jumped up and ran out. We carried on. Her cat was fine.

As my unconsciousness continued in a string of black bead-like moments, I was missing more and more of the reading. I could no longer hear most of what Delany was saying. Something about pirates, funny and dreadful at the same time. Something bloody, or uncomfortably sexual, or . . . I decided I would go to the bathroom and splash some water on my face, take a little stroll through the café, where some of Delany's already-established writer friends were hanging out, drinking beer, and listening through the open doorway. They would take him out later.

Standing up turned out to be a big mistake. I made it out of the reading before losing consciousness entirely. I hit the floor like a sack of horseshoes.

Luckily, Jane Hawkins, a member of the science-fiction community, was also hanging out in the café, and realized I was in trouble. She saw me sway and threw herself under me. I probably would have broken my nose otherwise. Jane might have tossed aside a glass of water before doing so.

The people in the café were on their feet by the time I came to. Jane had disentangled herself and was telling me to eat salt. Leslie Howle, the Clarion classroom coordinator, mother hen, and later director, was showing me where to apply acupressure to my hands to keep from passing out. Why do people always show you these things after the fact?

It happened so quickly that I don't think most people in the reading, sitting with their backs to us, noticed. I suppose I drove home and went to bed. At least I hope I did.

After that evening, they brought in big fans for hot nights in the Elliott Bay basement. Karen Maeda Allman or Rick Simonson would get up and introduce writers and encourage the audience to take breaks and drink lots of water. This, of course, led to the purchase of lots of beer and cheesecake along with books.

I attended many readings after that, by the famous, the infamous, and someday to be famous. Sometimes the readings were intimate, just a few friends who loved books. Others were epic, such as the Day of the Dead readings staged by the writers group Los Norteños in the early '90s. Sometimes I pushed myself out the door in support of a visiting writer who might not have a big Seattle readership, to find the crowd standing-room only. Eventually, the audience was there for my first book, a sweet moment, and way more fun than passing out.

Every summer, students still gather from all over the world to attend the Clarion West workshop. I even taught there one summer. Like everything else, it has become more competitive to attend. The weekly readings have moved to University Book Store, closer to classrooms and accommodations. Every July, Greg and Astrid Anderson Bear invite the students over to their house to meet a few local authors and listen to "The Talk" that Greg gives them about the world of publishing. They are sleepy. They are hungry. And they look so young. This marks the twenty-first year of continuous workshops.

I've never passed out during a reading since, and as far as I know, neither has anyone else. All in all, I gained more consciousness than I lost in the basement of the Elliott Bay Book Company.

STESHA BRANDON
Program Director, Town Hall

SOME OF THE MEMORABLE VISITING WRITERS WHO'VE TAKEN THE STAGE AT TOWN HALL

We have had the pleasure of hosting some phenomenal people: Cornel West brings down the house every time he speaks here. Colum McCann convinced his audience to read Joyce's *Ulysses*. Nicholson Baker is one of my all-time favorite philosopher/novelists. And Margaret Atwood is amazing; she's erudite and sarcastic and hilarious all at once.

VAMPIRE-RELATED QUESTIONS ARE WELCOME

My favorite recent interaction happened at a program with the wonderful Karen Russell. She was reading from *Vampires in the Lemon Grove*, and a young girl, maybe about thirteen, attended the program with her dad. She got up during the Q&A to ask Karen about vampires—how Karen decided what magical properties the vampires should have, and how those compared to other vampires in literature.

THE ONE BOOK BY A SEATTLEITE TO PUT IN THE HANDS OF A VISITOR

There are so many amazing Seattle writers, writing really different kinds of books. There are tons of great science writers living here: David Montgomery, David B. Williams, Lyanda Lynn Haupt.

Lyanda's books (like *Crow Planet* and *The Urban Bestiary*) shed light on Seattle's relationship with the wild. That said, the book that I can't stop raving about right now is Nicola Griffith's *Hild*. It's the story of the girl who will become Saint Hilda of Whitby, set against the power struggles and seismic shifts in religious belief of seventh-century Northumbria. It's a remarkable book—both accessible and erudite, beautifully crafted and well paced. You've got to read it!

SEATTLE WRITER WHO DESERVES MORE ATTENTION

I am an evangelist for Matthew Simmons. Matthew is a friend who happens to be a prodigiously talented writer. He is interested in pushing the form, and his writing also has a certain vulnerability. I think he's amazing and can't wait to see what he's going to do next!

BEST LITERARY PERFORMER

I would say Sherman Alexie. He's hilarious, and you never know what he'll say next. If we're talking about Washington writers, I have a fondness for Tom Robbins, as he so deftly conveys the pathos and humor of his books to his audiences. If we're talking about authors from across the United States, I was absolutely captivated by Cynthia Ozick's reading back in 2005, and I still hold that as the standard for reading fiction aloud. And if we're talking international authors, I absolutely adore Eoin Colfer. He puts every bit of himself into his performances.

BEST NEIGHBORHOOD TO SET A MURDER MYSTERY

I think a classic locked-room mystery set in and around the water tower in Volunteer Park is a given.

BEST NEIGHBORHOOD TO SET A SCIENCE-FICTION NOVEL

Maybe a postapocalyptic sci-fi novel could be set on the beaches at Lincoln Park, and on the Vashon ferry, which is set adrift between the island and mainland.

NEIGHBORHOOD BOOKSTORE OF CHOICE

I find myself shopping in the Elliott Bay Book Company the most often these days. I bought David Mitchell's *The Bone Clocks* and Rebecca Hoogs's poetry collection *Self-Storage* there just last week. But I like to spread the love, and I've shopped at University Book Store and Phinney Books in the last month or so too!

BEST DAY JOB FOR A WRITER IN SEATTLE

Writing? Is that a trick question? ;)

TOM NISSLEY

ON MARILYNNE ROBINSON,
DAVID FOSTER WALLACE, GRANT
COGSWELL, AND COFFEE SHOPS

I moved to Seattle to follow a writer who had left there long before. It's a story I've told so often it's pat, but really, it was pat to begin with. I chose the University of Washington for grad school in English for three reasons: I didn't get in anywhere else; I had been to Seattle in the summertime and liked it; and, most importantly, Marilynne Robinson, author of *Housekeeping*, had gotten her PhD in English at the UW, and had started writing *Housekeeping* there when she should have been working on her dissertation. If *she* did it, I said to myself, how wrong could I go? Really, that was the full extent of how I made, at age twenty-four, a decision from which everything else has followed. In retrospect, I think it was a good one.

I remember where I was when I heard that Dan Orozco, my friend and fellow UW grad student, had made *The Best American Short Stories 1995* for his story "Orientation." I was in the basement of Padelford, the UW English building, in the common room where the TAs made copies of our handouts before class. It was the perfect place—anxious with shared aspirations—to get that news. I had until then felt an insuperable gap between the private world of my writing and that of my friends on one hand, and the public, published world of books and magazines on the other, and this felt like the first time the two had been connected. That it was for "Orientation," which I had heard Dan read in his wry, patient cadence at the UW's Castalia series—maybe on the same night I read a lesser story—and which was easily the best story someone I knew I had written, made the connection seem authentic. The gatekeepers of the literary world had recognized the same thing that we out in the grad-school provinces already knew. Our best was everyone's best.

I have a far longer—and perhaps richer—life as a reader in Seattle than as a writer, a life that has had a few particularly intense loci over the years: the new-arrivals window display at Magus Books (and, around the corner on the Ave, the magazine racks at Bulldog News), the paperback new-releases tables at Bailey/Coy Books, the stacks and study tables in Suzzallo Library, and, of course, the Elliott Bay Book Company. Being a reader, for me, has always carried with it the undertones of wanting to be a writer, and going to Elliott Bay always brought out those undertones in their full ambivalence. The sublime pleasure of browsing through their encyclopedic stacks, especially the fiction section to which I aspired (and still aspire!), was often pervaded by a shapeless horror at all the new books that kept being released. How could all those books—much less my unpublished (and unwritten) ones—hope to find readers?

And every time I sat down on one of the narrow, barely cushioned round wooden chairs at a reading in the store's original brick basement, I was conscious of the hope that someday I would read from a book of my own there. (Reader, I did, although only after they moved to Capitol Hill.) I'm sure we all have our lists of memorable evenings from the thousands the store has hosted over the years—my own list includes packed houses for Dorothy Allison, John Edgar Wideman, and Junot Díaz, the night Jonathan Franzen expressed complexity about *The Corrections* being chosen by Oprah, and the night William Vollmann laid down a gun on the lectern at the beginning of his reading and then, far enough into his story that we had forgotten about it, picked up the weapon and shot off a blank.

But one evening there stands out in particular: when David Foster Wallace read from *Infinite Jest*. I remember being a little skeptical that someone so promising had written a book so unreadably immense, but he won me over: his reading of the video telephony section of the novel had everyone in the room losing their breath in laughter, to the point that Dave himself had to pause because, in endearing Harvey Korman style, he was cracking himself up too much to continue. But after the reading, the spell broke: As I remember it, he left the podium and was met halfway by the bookseller who had introduced him, and who reminded him that there was also to be an audience Q&A. He wasn't thrilled about the idea, and for an uncomfortable moment they stood there, neither on the stage nor off it, until someone threw out a question from the crowd, to which Wallace said, "If that's what they're going to be like, I don't think so." And that was that. (I always feel obligated, though, to follow that story by saying that DFW came back to town a few years later to give a seminar at the UW, bandanna and tobacco spit cup, and all, and was engaged and brilliant and not dismissive of his crowd of questioners in the least.)

I'm sure Seattle remembers Grant Cogswell best as a political gadfly who came bewilderingly close to getting things done—like expanding the monorail and getting elected to City Council—or maybe as a filmmaker who made, by his own estimation, a terrible Seattle-produced movie called *Cthulhu*. But his many passions and talents—his passion being one of his greatest talents—include writing and reading too. My fondest Grant moment—and the one that really connected me to him for the first time, and perhaps vice versa—was when, to honor the recent death of the poet A. R. Ammons, he organized at Victrola Coffee a many-hour reading of Ammons's book-length poem *Sphere*, a poem I loved but, until, then had imagined I was the only person in Seattle to have read. I don't know how he organized it or how I heard about it, I don't remember who else was there, and I don't remember what part I read, but at the time—and even more so now—it felt like a moment so beautifully singular and appropriate that it could only have come down from the heavens, or from the mind of Grant Cogswell.

It's a cliché that Seattle is the city of coffee shops, and it's a cliché that coffee shops are full of writers nursing their lattes, but for me that cliché is a fully embodied truth, and I want to pay tribute to a small public space that meant everything to me for a few years. When I had a busy job and two little kids and, it seemed, no prospect of a moment to myself, I worked it out to start spending a few hours out on my own every Sunday afternoon.

The best place I found to do that was in the narrow little upper-floor section of Peet's Coffee & Tea at the north end of the Fremont Bridge. Somehow it was the ideal space for what I needed: no Wi-Fi, good pots of tea I could sip long after they got cold, a somewhat-diverting view of Dusty Strings and the other businesses across Fremont Avenue, and just enough activity that there was often a good conversation to overhear but not so much that I couldn't get a seat near one of the two outlets. At first, I just went there every week to read and observe and be alone with my thoughts for a change, but soon I began to write. It may be that no one will ever read much of what I wrote there, but it was better than anything I had written before, and the space felt like it had something to do with that. That Peet's location closed after its lease got too expensive, and was replaced by a Starbucks, to whose upper floor I've begun to return. The aprons and the tea and the corporate overseers have changed, but the space is—almost—the same.

ELI HASTINGS

ON PONGO

I came of age in '90s Seattle, when "culture" was oozing out of grimy clubs, bookstores, and coffee shops. My mother lived a stone's throw from the house where Kurt Cobain ended his suffering. We used to smoke pot in the early morning hours on the top floor of Cafe Paradiso (now Caffe Vita) on Pike. I tried to read the *Rocket* sometimes. But all of that is background noise. Here's the truth: I went to Washington Middle School and then Garfield High School. And while bohemian Seattle's veins were running with grunge and poetry (Jesse Bernstein threatening to cut off his cock in Pioneer Square, and Cobain starting to sing dark, catchy shit in smoky back rooms), even us white boys lived mainly within black culture, despite the racial divisions. We were happily oblivious, haunting city parks with forty-ounce bottles of Mickey's Ice (the white-boy equivalent of Olde English), listening to A Tribe Called Quest, De La Soul, and a whole lot of Led Zeppelin. There was no musical or literary scene proffered to the minors of Seattle, at least minors who found themselves being forged by inner-city education. (In my case, the decision of a progressive mother who thought I ought to be getting a "social education"—I have since learned that what she'd intended was not quite what I received, but I have no regrets.)

Still, that didn't keep me from writing. Thousands of pages of horrific purple prose in leather-bound journals. After a while, I was likely to slip out of a weed circle and go scribble away.

Fast-forward thirteen years and I've got an MFA in creative non-fiction, a father who died too young, a best friend who ended up blown out by some Belltown smack in a goddamn alley, one published book, three expatriate years of living warm and dry and strange in Barcelona, and just enough nostalgia, faith, and loyalty to come home.

One thing I knew for sure: writing had saved my life when grief and trauma tried to take it. And this was something that I had to pay forward. And I wanted to pay it forward in large part to the communities that don't make it into anthologies of Seattle writers or attend poetry readings on Capitol Hill. So I jumped into Writers in the Schools, started running workshops at a domestic violence shelter, cobbled together other gigs, and undertook what I magnanimously thought of as "feasibility study" to figure out how to bring creative writing to the underserved.

One gray spring morning, I parked outside a coffee shop where I was to meet a young woman from Pat Graney's theater group for a consultation. I stayed in the car, making myself a bit tardy, because KPLU was airing a piece on the work that some bizarre little nonprofit called Pongo was doing in a children's psychiatric unit downstate and at King County Juvenile Detention. It was riveting and inspiring. Over our lattes, the young woman listened to my vague, idealistic notions. One of the first things she said to me was, "You should talk to Richard Gold." Richard Gold, of course, had been speaking through the shot speakers of my truck just moments before about his organization, Pongo.

It took me less than an hour to get Richard on the phone, listening to me spew about my absolute determination to help heal through writing, but that didn't mean that I got to skip the painstaking process to become a Pongo mentor: two interviews, extensive background checks (and attendant explanations), orientation to the Youth Services Center (read "juvie"), and intensive training in the methodology that Pongo uses.

I've spent six years with Pongo now, as a poetry mentor, project leader, consultant, and assistant director. Any "Pongoite" (as we call each other without any irony) can bury you in breathtaking anecdotes. Finally, after nearly twenty years—having served some seven thousand kids, published a dozen volumes of their work, and spread their voices to tens of thousands of people who wouldn't normally hear them or give a second thought to a "disturbed" or "thuggish" kid—Pongo has started to get proper recognition through awards, documentaries, and publications. I'll just share two memories of my "literary Seattle," that are, as they must be, also Pongo anecdotes.

Every Tuesday from September through April for many years, I worked my way through the various layers of security at King County Juvenile Detention: past the bored but friendly Filipinos manning the X-Ray and metal detectors; past the slumped, chatting sheriff's deputies at the entrance to the courtrooms; down the stairs and through the sally port, after exchanging ID for visitor badge; down another hallway and flight of stairs, to sign in at security post one and ultimately settle into a dorm. Every week we have the chance to pull two groups of youth from their interagency school, which occupies the north end of the facility. We almost never have any trouble getting enough eager writers; we often have trouble turning down those we can't accommodate.

This particular year, there was a gray-eyed blonde pixie of a girl that stood under five feet tall and was thirteen years of age. She existed on the periphery of the eye-rolling, smack-talking personalities of the majority of female students. A staff person urged us to encourage her to try Pongo, and we did so—several weeks in a row. With a mumble, a shake of her head, and an apologetic air, she always turned us down. Until she didn't. I don't know why she changed her mind or why she chose my two-hundred-pound rubber table to sit at once we were back in the dorm, but I was excited that our overtures had worked.

She turned poetry books around in her tiny hands and avoided my eyes and responded monosyllabically for a few minutes before I essentially insisted that we get started. That's when she admitted to me that she was so severely dyslexic she couldn't read or write. One of the great graces of Pongo is that this doesn't actually matter, and after I'd convinced her of this, her eyes lifted to mine and her spine straightened some and she allowed that she wouldn't mind writing a letter to her mother. I issued her the prompt *I just thought you should know*, and this is what she dictated:

Dear Mom,

I just thought you should know what I'm doing now. I'm addicted to drugs and in juvie a lot. I am an unloved person who spends a lot of time doing drugs to feel better and not abandoned.

I just thought you should know how I'm feeling. I just hate you. I hate my dad too. I hate you because you left me one night when I was seven and never came back. The police broke down the door to take me to foster care. But even before that, you brought home men who hurt me and did bad things to me. I hate you for pimping me out. I hate you for packing my nose full of white powder, which is why I have breathing problems now. I hate you for getting me into drugs. I hate you because I ended up in a gang. I hate you.

I just thought you should know what I've been through. Since the last time I saw you, I've been in more foster homes than I can count but 45 to 50 percent of them were abusive. I always run, but the system found me, didn't believe me, and put me in another, and another. The time that I was going to be adopted was especially important. They came and picked me, and I lived in their house for a week before they found about my history and they sent me back.

I just thought you should know what I wish for the future. I hope that somehow I can yell at you without having to see you, to blame all this crap on you. Though it would do nothing for me, at least I wouldn't have to hold it inside any longer.

I just thought you should know what I don't miss about
you . . . I don't miss you at all.
    I'm glad I don't have to worry about you leaving me again
and not coming back.
    I just thought you should know that there is nothing at all
that I miss about you.
    I just thought you should know that no matter what, you'll
always be my mom and I'll always love you.

Before she gave me the last line, she paused, and fat dollops of
tears escaped her eyes; her brain seemed stuck, like a computer
with too many programs open.

"What is it?" I asked. "What were you going to say?"

"It doesn't make any sense," she whispered.

But then she said it anyway. And she dedicated the poem to
her mother.

She smiled and cried as I read it back to her and, I heard later,
she shared it with her class, who applauded her. She came back and
wrote with us several more times, and her poem will be published
in the next anthology of voices.

In 2010, I accepted a residency with the Seattle Arts & Lectures
Writers in the Schools program, because they wanted to send
me back to my alma mater. It probably shouldn't have surprised
me that certain things hadn't changed much. The renovations at
Garfield were impressive, and the Quincy Jones Performance
Center was especially so. The same team was running security (and
yes, they recognized me, amused) but now with the addition of a

big, friendly cop at the front door. And kids were definitely not running as wild—truancy was a concept that had been brought back into relevance, apparently. But the racial divisions with their academic reflections were more in place than ever.

I was given three periods of "Garfield Preparatory Academy," which turned out to be a euphemism for "bad kids," 97 percent of whom were black or Latino. The teachers I worked with ranged from well-intentioned but ineffectual to cheerfully apathetic. On the one hand, I wanted desperately to spark the students' passion and cause them to react against the pigeonhole I could see them so obviously thrust into; on the other, I understood that many of them had simply thrown in the towel long ago and learned how to execute the bare minimum to scrape by in a system that has a vested interest in seeing them graduate, whether or not they find themselves prepared for higher education or life in general.

At any given moment, there were kids chatting on their cell phones, chasing one another, eating takeout, and throwing various (sometimes dangerous) items at each other while shouting obscenities and racial slurs. Needless to say, facilitating a discussion on rhyme schemes in this context is a laughable enterprise, to say nothing of building a tranquil and safe enough space for kids to share their work.

I suspected that sharing the voices of their peers (most Pongo authors fall in the age range of my students and come from the same neighborhoods) would challenge my students' ability to remain "cool," dismissive, superficial, *loud*. It turned out I was right—the renderings of deep pain and trauma silenced the classes. When I read "The Guy with the Green Eyes" by a sixteen-year-old, you could have heard a cell phone vibrate:

He made me do things I didn't want to do?
by threatening the life of my little brother?
with a shotgun

I watched one of the preeminent class clowns break open an imaginary shotgun with a guffaw, only to be stared into silence by the very girls he was trying to impress. After the reading, I laid out an array of Pongo prompts, and it was only twenty minutes before I reaped the largest crop of quality writing I'd yet received, including accounts of struggles with sexual orientation, suicidal ideation, and the personal impact of the racist educational system they were folded harshly into.

More importantly, maybe, was the fact that after that day, things changed. After that day, we had hard group discussions about racism in education and in the community, about the silly masculine mandates to always appear indifferent, and about the hypocrisy inherent in one underserved or oppressed group dissing another.

There is an impressive historical record of literature in Seattle, from Richard Hugo to today's increasingly iconic geniuses (and friends of mine) like Peter Mountford, Garth Stein, Tess Gallagher, and many more. There are also scrappy and deeply courageous people and programs putting in work to bring out the voices of young people who aren't often heard. That tradition is deeply Seattle too.

Keep an ear open for it.

PAM CADY

Manager, University Book Store

●▬▬➤ ●▬▬➤ ●▬▬➤

MOST MEMORABLE VISITING WRITER

A few years ago, just after *Fun Home* came out, we had an event with Alison Bechdel. She's fairly shy, but she's an amazing public speaker. She narrated this terrific slide show she put together of her life and work. The place was so mobbed I was getting super-nervous that we would have to turn people away, but somehow people squeezed into every little crevice that was available. So we had about 300 people in a space that fits, at most, 175. It was hot, and no one had any personal space, but no one cared. The signing line was full of local artists and lesbians. It took a long time to wind down. I noticed that three young women were waiting for the signing to end so they could be the last ones to talk to Alison. They were groupies, and they were very rakish and attractive. Finally, one of them looked around real quick to make sure everyone else had left, pulled her pants down, and asked Alison to sign her boxers. I can remember heartily approving of the design of the boxers, but Alison and I just stood there kind of gaping at this turn of events. Finally, we looked at each other and decided, well, why not sign them? So she ended up signing one pair of boxers and one bra.

MOST RIDICULOUS QUESTION A CUSTOMER EVER ASKED

Remember when *Women Who Run With the Wolves* by Clarissa Pinkola Estés was popular? A man came into the store and asked where we kept the book *Women Who Swim With the Whales*. Of course, it felt almost as ridiculous saying, "I think what you really want is *Women Who Run With the Wolves*."

One year during the holidays, we had a display of expensive art books. I saw a customer put a wet drink down on top of a two-hundred-dollar book. I asked him politely if he would remove it. The guy looked at me with outrage and said, "Oh, quit your f'ing book morality." And then he grabbed his drink and stormed out. Merry Christmas!

BEST LITERARY PERFORMER

Jonathan Evison is not only one of my favorite people on the planet, but he's just entirely entertaining. And he's also one of the most warm-hearted guys. Garth Stein tells the best stories, Sherman Alexie has charisma oozing out of his ears, and Maria Semple is hilarious once you get her going. And Ivan Doig. My coworker, Brad Craft, said that he could have listened to Ivan read to him all night.

THE ONE BOOK BY A SEATTLEITE TO PUT
IN THE HANDS OF A VISITOR

Just about everyday I put *The Boys in the Boat* by Daniel James Brown into someone's hands. No one has ever been disappointed as far as I know.

SEATTLE WRITER WHOSE NEXT BOOK WE
SHOULD ALL LOOK FORWARD TO

Thor Hanson's, because who else is going to get me to read about feathers, seeds, and gorillas? I have no idea what he's doing next, but he's so good that I'll have to read it. I think he's becoming Seattle's John McPhee.

PART 3

WORKING

LESLEY HAZELTON

ON WHERE SHE WRITES

Sometimes I wonder how much more I'd get done if I didn't live on the water. Forty feet of it, to be precise. But I resist counting words. Living on a raft five minutes north of downtown goes beyond productivity.

It's a mobile home, really. A two-room houseboat so torqued by wind and wakes that not a true ninety-degree angle has survived, it retains its essential shackiness, woodstove and all. The upscale term for it is "floating home," a *Better Homes and Gardens* designation that would have had the logger who threw it together a hundred years back derisively snorting his beer into the lake. Commonly, it's known as unreal estate. I think the logger would break out another beer for that.

I spend a lot of time sitting at my desk and gazing out the window. Not at anything in particular, just the water, always in motion. Like thought, like words. Glinting silver and black and that steely gray that romantics call blue, it changes shape at the slightest excuse, gathering into cats' paws, riffles, waves, even whitecaps on a stormy day.

Some feel insecure here, unrooted. All this fluidity makes them nervous. To me, it's essential. After twenty-odd years on the raft, I get restless on land, miss the awareness of water never being in the same place twice. The world seems oddly silent without the thrum of rain on the surface, the flurry of ducks landing, the roar of a floatplane on takeoff. And less welcoming if I can't dive in on a hot summer day or float in dark silkiness on a calm moonless night. Work, play, and life all swirl together here, all in motion. Like words.

GARTH STEIN

ON WHERE HE WRITES

I used to like to write in the spare bedroom in my house, which is tucked away in a lovely urban-woodsy Brooklyn-ish neighborhood between Beacon Hill and Lake Washington. We have a nice brick house, three stories tall, perched precariously on a steep grade alive with pine trees and oak trees, and home to a ninety-year-old laurel bush that looms thirty feet high and stretches fifty feet from one end to the other between our house and our neighbor's—seriously, this is *one* plant, with a trunk thirty-six inches in circumference. Like they make in Brobdingnag.

The house was built in 1924 and has a peek-a-boo view of Lake Washington. We're across from a park, which, like almost all of the older parks in Seattle, was designed by the Olmsted Brothers around the turn of the twentieth century. The old trees on the drive below our house bend over the road and form a mall of leaves in the summer, like you would see in a French film. And when you're on the top floor of our house and look out to the park, if feels like you're in a tree house.

I loved writing in that back bedroom; I wrote my second novel there. But I also loved it because it provided me the perfect excuse not to write. (The easiest thing to do in the *world* is not write!) I could invent the need to cook an elaborate dinner, for instance. Or cite my sons' sudden need to learn to throw a baseball. Almost anything would do.

But then one day, my wife walked into my office while I was writing. She carefully sized up the layout, ticking items off in her head. "I think we'll put the crib *there*," she said. We had two sons, eight and ten; now we were having a third. And I was being evicted.

I found a little apartment just down the street from us, also overlooking the boulevard. That was a good place to write too. But it was short-lived solution. The owners converted it to a condo, and I was evicted again.

I wandered the coffee shops, hoping to find salvation as an itinerant writer. Victrola. Bauhaus. Caffe Vita. Yes, even Starbucks. But I never took to coffeehouse writing. I was too worried about having to pee after drinking so much coffee that my hands shook, and the inevitable next question: Should I leave my computer at a table and ask someone to look after it, or should I pack up and go to the restroom and then change locations? It was very disconcerting to me.

Then I drove through a neighborhood just south of us called Columbia City. It used to be its own city before Seattle grew up around it and swallowed it whole. In the nineteenth century, it had its own train station and a lumber mill. The old movie theater is still there. Yet the neighborhood had no office vacancy.

Rob Mohn, one of the local developers in Columbia City, told me to check with a guy named Joe Fugere who had just opened a pizza restaurant and was using a loft above the Columbia City Ale House as his support office. It was too much space, and he was thinking of bringing in some freelancers to fill out the floor.

Well, that was just perfect. Joe was the nicest guy in the world. His pizza was great. And I had a new place to work.

I loved working in the offices of Tutta Bella Neapolitan Pizzeria, mostly because the folks there treated me like I was one of them. They all had jobs. They were general managers and accountants and marketing people. I didn't have a job. I was a guy in the cubicle in the back who wore headphones to blot out the sound and could sometimes be heard acting out dialogue from a scene in his book.

"Who's that?" a vendor or a guest might ask.

"Oh, him? He's a writer. Don't worry about him."

I wrote *The Art of Racing in the Rain* there. People sometimes ask me if I cry when I write an emotional scene. I do. The fine people at Tutta Bella will verify that fact.

I was with Tutta Bella for seven years. I didn't want to leave, and Joe didn't want me to go. But his pizza place had grown into a family of five restaurants, and he needed my desk for his business. The other freelancers had all moved on, but I had become somewhat of a mascot, I like to think. The hardworking writer who hit it big with a novel written, edited, and marketed entirely under their roof. Still, I knew it was time. And besides, Joe had charged me almost no rent for seven years; I could afford an office of my own.

So I took off for Georgetown, a stubbornly industrial fringe neighborhood mashed between I-5, a phalanx of railroad tracks, and the north end of Boeing Field. I have a loft in an old beer brewery that's been taken over by artists. I eat falafel from a food truck and some of the best pho in Seattle from a little place in a strip mall a few blocks away, and I eat some of the best Mexican food I've ever tasted from the restaurant across Airport Way. I have no air-conditioning, so in the hot weeks of summer I practice what I call "Bikram Hot Writing" in my baking top-floor office with three fans pointed at my face. I stand at my sit-to-stand desk and sweat and write books. I've written another book here, in this place. The trains are frighteningly loud when they use the spur a hundred feet from my window to change tracks. The horns and the clacking and the shrieking of brakes. And the airplanes. When Boeing tests a Dreamliner, it thunders over Georgetown, so my windows rattle and I look out at the blue belly that's so close I feel I can touch it. That's when I love where I am so much. Because I am alone. I have no phone here. I am anonymous. If I want to turn off my Wi-Fi, I can. Then I am unreachable. But I do not feel alone, because I always know civilization is just outside my old, leaky windows and just above my whitewashed wood ceiling.

Location plays a big role in my writing; it's another character. I write about Seattle: the places where I grew up, the places I hung out and explored, the places I've lived. But as much as Seattle has informed what I've written about, it also informs *how* I write.

This is a city of neighborhoods, each with its own personality. Wherever a writer finds a place to perch is a good place to write. For me, I've moved from our upstairs bedroom to the Tutta Bella support offices in Columbia City to my loft in Georgetown, and I've felt the energy of each place seep into my bones and infuse my writing with something unique. I recognize that each of the three books I've written in Seattle has taken on some of the distinctiveness of the place it was written. The reader may not see it, but I do. I don't want to move again to write another novel, but I know that if I do have to, there will always be another perfect writing spot in Seattle for me to find.

JANIS SEGRESS

Manager/Co-Owner, Queen Anne Book Company

ONE BOOK TO *NOT* RECOMMEND

I wasn't a fan of Stieg Larsson from the get-go. I read a galley after it hit big in Europe and was due to the United States. I was so disgusted I ripped my galley in half. I told one of my best customers at the time not to waste their money on the preorder. Obviously, the series went on to do enormously well in sales in the United States. However, I stand by my initial gut read.

GOOD ADVICE FROM GARTH STEIN

I took a short-story class from Garth Stein back in 2010 through the Field's End writers' community. It went quite well; I learned a lot. I was especially intrigued by Garth's comment on my short-short story, ". . . watch the snarkiness."

**THE ONE BOOK BY A SEATTLEITE TO PUT
IN THE HANDS OF A VISITOR**

The Boys in the Boat by Daniel James Brown. This work of narrative nonfiction is a masterful telling of an important piece of Washington State history. I think it is an overall testament to the integrity, resilience, and success that has always defined Seattle. Daniel James Brown takes the reader back to the Great Depression, immersing us in a realistic voice, and delivers the kind of victory story that is usually found in fiction. The University of Washington men's rowing team wins Olympic gold in Hitler's Germany. Inspirational, heroic, history-making.

SEATTLE WRITER WHO DESERVES MORE ATTENTION

Joe Guppy, author of *My Fluorescent God*. Guppy has been a journalist, theater and television performer, and psychotherapist, and he's experienced drug-induced paranoid psychosis. I was amazed at Guppy's ability, as a first-time author, to render a highly personal story into one that reaches out with compassion and truth, and pulls the reader in for a unique experience.

BEST LITERARY PERFORMER

Sherman Alexie, hands down. When an author actually publishes a book, usually after eons of extreme exertion, they soon learn that part of the role is public speaking. Sherman goes beyond the "presenter" role and is truly a natural and gifted performer. In fact, he is the epitome of the intellectual, smart-ass, stand-up comedy genre. He assesses his audience and adjusts his presentation with perfection. Hollywood, watch out.

BEST NEIGHBORHOOD TO SET A MURDER MYSTERY

Capitol Hill—on Broadway, to be exact—is the perfect place to set a mystery. It is literally teeming with characters, with rotating scenes within scenes. All five senses are alerted, and sometimes attacked, at once.

BEST NEIGHBORHOOD TO SET A SCIENCE-FICTION NOVEL

Most definitely the lovely Laurelhurst, where a time ladder leads from the early 1800s to 2015. Laurelhurst has never really been what it pretends to be. It was originally Sahlouwil, the campground of the Duwamish Indians. This could be a fantastic story. If someone steals it, they read it here first.

MOST RIDICULOUS QUESTION A CUSTOMER EVER ASKED

"I'm looking for a book . . . I don't remember the title, or the author. Or if it is nonfiction, or fiction, or adult or children's. I really don't remember where I heard about it, or when. But—it has the word 'water' in the title!"

BEST DAY JOB FOR A WRITER IN SEATTLE

Bookseller at an independent bookstore.

STACEY LEVINE

ON WRITING IN PUBLIC

Each year has nine gray months, and I love them. Seasonal affective disorder hasn't hit me so far, and the spattery, misty winter isn't a pain but a blurry pleasure. It sounds like jazz piano, and in the city there are so many places to write. Who needs to haul out to a writers' retreat in the woods far away from home, in tense proximity to other moody writers? I like writing in Seattle, and often after teaching I look for urban, public places with a little buzz of background noise where I can write with little distraction; sometimes the ideal public workspace evades me and sometimes not.

While working on one book, I spent time regularly at World Pizza in the International District, which has unbelievably strong and balanced espresso and the friendliest owners. During nonlunch hours while the city is layered in rain, it's dreamy to sit in one of World Pizza's wooden booths and work for a few hours.

Another spot with low-key background noise is Dur Dur Café on Cherry Street near Twenty-Third, famous in the neighborhood for its peppery chai, which has been roughly a dollar a cup for at least ten years. This tonic is good on cold, sleepy afternoons and Dur Dur's minimal decor makes it easy to focus on work. It's also the only spot I'm aware of in our far-north city that serves lunch entrées with a side of banana.

Caffe Vita on Capitol Hill is an excellent work spot in the winter, with terrific, well-considered music and a Seattle aloof-friendliness that makes it a great spot for work; besides, Vita's ice water is pure and fantastic. Here, as with most Seattle cafés, you'll never be made to feel like a jerk for ordering only tea with many subsequent cups of hot water.

Both of the above cafés are quieter than the University of Washington's Odegaard Library: its main floor has the din of a shopping mall. But Odegaard's top floor, a dedicated silent space popular with students, some faculty, and random townsfolk, is a place where no one greets or even glances at anyone else. For me, this socially chilly atmosphere is perfect for writing. As well, the UW law library is strictly silent—cell phones off, no speaking allowed. When library users talk too loudly at this place, the librarians tend to come out from their desks and verbally bash them. Heaven.

There's also the Scandiuzzi Writers' Room in Seattle's downtown Central Library, a beautiful haven. It's on the ninth floor beside the library's upper spiral, and from it you can look out at the skyline through the diagonal steel-and-glass wrap that swathes the building. You can watch the rain roll on the glass and fall, the endless plenty of it.

To use this room, writers must submit an application, and be approved by library staff, but the brief process is worth it. It's a near-silent space, with ergonomic clean-line desks. It's funny that the Writers' Room is also positioned just below the library's highest lookout point. I've often worked in the Writers' Room and glanced up to see tourists taking pictures of the writers hunched at their desks in the space. The tourists point and wave. Once in the room with me sat the droll and deep Seattle writer/performer Curtis Taylor, grinning as we were being watched, and he said: "This place is a little bit like a holding pen." But the high-up Scandiuzzi room is my favorite public spot for writing in Seattle, I told him, and I like the simple, scary act of holding a pen.

JAMES CROSSLEY
Bookseller, Island Books

A COMIC WHO LOVED COMICS

Robin Williams came in and spent at least thirty minutes shopping for graphic novels. We spent at least half that time talking about comics, about which he was very knowledgeable, and he couldn't have been nicer. He bought several books, although I don't remember which ones. I do remember what he didn't buy, which was *In the Shadow of No Towers*, Art Spiegelman's response to the 9/11 attacks. He was really excited to hear about it, and I had copies in the back of the store, but it wouldn't be released officially for another day or two, so I didn't bring one out for him. I feel worse about that every time I think of it.

MOST RIDICULOUS QUESTION A CUSTOMER EVER ASKED

One of the most ridiculous moments came when a customer walked into my old shop on the busiest street in the most left-wing neighborhood of the most left-wing city in the most left-wing state in the country and asked why we were censoring Ann Coulter and Rush Limbaugh by not having any of their books in the store. That guy knows more now about capitalism and the First Amendment than he did when he walked in, I promise. More recently, I was asked by a young girl, "What is lard?" Oracles of all knowledge, we bookstore clerks are. My favorite question came over the phone: "Do you have any Sea-Monkey food?" That one actually made it into *Weird Things Customers Say in Bookstores* by Jen Campbell.

THE ONE BOOK BY A SEATTLEITE TO PUT IN THE HANDS OF A VISITOR

I'm tempted to choose *Gravity's Rainbow*, my favorite Thomas Pynchon novel, one that remains as mind-bogglingly impressive today as it did forty years ago, though I doubt very many people will agree with my calling Pynchon a Seattle writer. But, hey, he lived here for at least a couple of years and apparently wrote most or all of his novel *V.* in the city. Who cares if he's said to have referred to Seattle as "a nightmare" and fled to Mexico right after finishing it? Maria Semple's epistolary comedy *Where'd You Go, Bernadette* is one of the few books I know that directly addresses some of the Seattle-specific idiosyncrasies that out-of-town visitors should know about, like our inability to cope efficiently with intersections having multiple stop signs. Then there are the Seattle sections of the *U.S.A.* trilogy by John Dos Passos—can I count those? Readers shouldn't neglect more straightforward histories either, particularly Murray Morgan's *Skid Road*, Bill Speidel's *Sons of the Profits*, or Coll Thrush's *Native Seattle*. Oh, and this hypothetical out-of-towner should know about our great local science-fiction scene, so maybe something by Frank Herbert, Octavia Butler, or Nicola Griffith.

BEST NEIGHBORHOOD TO SET A MURDER MYSTERY

If I'm going to read a murder mystery, I think I want it to have a histor-ical setting, full of cobbled streets and gaslit shadows. Pioneer Square would seem to be the obvious choice, probably too obvious. Better to start our story in Georgetown, still raffish and independent a hundred years after being annexed by its bigger, younger sibling, Seattle.

BEST NEIGHBORHOOD TO SET A SCIENCE-FICTION NOVEL

I'm pretty sure a number of cyberpunk dystopias have already been written about the yet-unbuilt corporate tech hub that's forming in South Lake Union. Those novels willed the neighborhood into being.

SEATTLE WRITER WHO DESERVES MORE ATTENTION

L. Timmel Duchamp, the author of much thoughtful speculative fiction, notably the five-volume Marq'ssan Cycle. The 2009 James Tiptree, Jr. Award jury gave it a special honor. She's also the founder of Aqueduct Press, which specializes in publishing feminist science fiction. The work she's championed there and made available to the world includes the unsettling *Dangerous Space* from local author Kelley Eskridge, and international writing that includes *Life* by Englishwoman Gwyneth Jones, reminiscent of the best novels from Nicholas Mosley and A. S. Byatt; and *Squaring the Circle* by Romanian Gheorghe Săsărman (translated by Ursula K. Le Guin), which stands on par with Italo Calvino's *Invisible Cities*. Truly terrible book covers on all of these, but don't tell Duchamp I said that.

BEST DAY JOB FOR A WRITER IN SEATTLE

Do they still have people working in those little towers on the drawbridges over the Ship Canal?

JIM LYNCH

ON WRITING IN A PARKING BOOTH

My first paid writing job required me to dress up like a cop and work out of a parking-garage booth on Alaskan Way near Pike Street.

The people who ran the Hillclimb Court Garage hoped they'd found somebody to work the least popular graveyard shift—4 p.m. Saturday to 4 a.m. Sunday. What they got was a partied-out UW senior who looked at those long hours and that three-foot-by-five-foot booth as the solitary confinement he needed.

It was early 1985, so my shift was almost entirely in the dark. During breaks, I'd roam Alaskan Way and soak up the street life. It was more despairing back then. There weren't upscale restaurants, much less a touristy Ferris wheel, nearby. After dark, the strip belonged to all the hobos and winos, as if they'd tumbled down the hills to the waterfront.

From the awkward vantage of a uniformed security guard, I watched them share bottles, laughter, and hostilities before passing out on the wharfs. My favorite hobo got hallucinatory after midnight. He'd occasionally bowl a frame or two beneath the Viaduct with his imaginary ball and lane. He had good form, a great follow-through.

I'd retreat to my booth and invent their backstories. It thrilled this suburban boy to think that if I watched closely enough I might describe a dark side of glamorous Seattle that most people never saw. I turned one bum into a prophet who spray-painted wisdom all along the Viaduct, which nobody read but everybody needed. Just writing the gritty, honest sentences made me feel like a young George Orwell or Henry Miller.

The scary part of the job involved patrolling two condominium complexes above the garage next to Pike Place Market. If I caught anybody in the act of anything, I looked like a cop, though I was just a minimum-wage security guard armed with just a long flash-light. Eventually, these rounds didn't seem worth the risks. For several shifts before I quit, I fabricated reports when I didn't feel the courage to patrol those dark stairways and rooftops.

Mostly, I hunched in that heated booth and wrote longhand through the night, as if on deadline, though I never shared any of those pages. I'd known for years that writing excited me, but it still surprised me how much I looked forward to that weekly shift. I was learning about myself. In that claustrophobic booth, I realized I'd continue to write no matter what I did for a living, and no matter what anybody else made of my words.

BHARTI KIRCHNER

ON TEACHING A WORKSHOP
AT A FERRY TERMINAL

Standing on the littered floor of the passenger waiting area of the Pier 69 ferry terminal, I introduced the topic for the class: writing about food memories of childhood. Ten or so mostly middle-aged people, seated in a loose group off to the side of the hall, barely looked up at me. I smelled greasy hot dogs and noted the constant stream of passengers hurrying past us. With the blare of departure announcements in the background, I began to have doubts about teaching an hour-long food-writing class in this facility.

My discomfort had started even before I arrived. Walking along the pier on Seattle's waterfront, I'd marveled at the Olympic Mountains and the white sailboats crossing the blue water of Puget Sound, the day around me a perfect Pacific Northwest autumn tableau. Before long, however, my view now blocked by buildings, I found myself passing tacky tourist shops, dodging broken glass, and avoiding panhandlers. Once again, I was reminded that this stretch of Alaskan Way could be a bit on the seamy side.

With everyone seemingly coming from somewhere else, and traffic noise so cacophonous that I could barely hear my own thoughts, it was impossible to feel at ease. Even I, a longtime resident of Seattle, a city I had come to call home, felt alienated.

But I had a class to teach. So, despite being in an unsettled state, I managed a smile and passed around a platter of homemade oatmeal-raisin cookies I'd brought.

The word "food" seemed to break the ice. Or maybe it was the cookies. Or even an attempt on my students' part to ease my evident discomfort with what might be considered an unusual classroom setting. For as soon as I gave them the writing prompt of jotting down a few words, phrases, or sentences about a childhood food experience, then asked them to share, many hands went up enthusiastically.

Jack, a tall bearded man, talked about his grandmother's cherry pie. "Her pies would smell so sweet that I'd coming running up from the basement where I'd be playing. But this one time she forgot the sugar. It was still good, because she had her signature almond flavoring in it. To this day, I can't go by a bakery without remembering Granny and her cherry pie."

Matthew, short and dark-haired, brimmed with excitement as he described a luscious peach obtained from a farmer's stand. "I was a cute kid, and a vendor just gave it to me. The peach was furry and juicy, with a blush like on a girl's cheeks."

There were smiles, nods, and mumblings of praise from the rest of the group, all except for Sandy, who silently kept picking out the raisins from her cookie.

Now I asked them to dig deeper into their food memories: What did that experience really mean to you? Why do you still remember it? And what can you pass on to others?

Jack finished scribbling and rubbed his beard. "It wasn't the pie. It was my granny, her bosomy hug, like she was going to surround me with warmth. She made me feel like I was at the center of things."

"That's the same way I felt when the guy at the fruit stand gave me a peach," Matthew said. "Like I was real special."

"Hey, guys, that's way cool," Ellen, dark-eyed and gaunt, said. "Better get that down on paper. We're writers now."

"Okay, but first tell us about what got *your* juices flowing," Jack said to Ellen.

Ellen adjusted her navy wool cap and seemed to struggle for a moment. Haltingly, she related her discovery of an unopened bag of potato chips while Dumpster-diving in the company of an emaciated stray dog. "I was so hungry I'd have eaten just about anything right then. And so would the dog. Sorry to say he didn't get even a single chip."

"Whatever was going on with you at the time," Jack said, "it's good material for you now, 'cause you're a writer."

I nodded. For writers they had become, these people who lived on the street, some of whom had shopping carts filled with their entire worldly possessions parked next to them.

They picked up their pens and hunched over their notebooks, leaving me to ponder the concept of home. As an émigré from India, I'd experienced intense feelings of homelessness myself and I was keenly aware of the need to feel secure and grounded, as I'd been in my motherland. Over the years, Seattle had fulfilled both those needs. In a sense, my writing had also given me a place to call home. Could it be that was why I felt compelled to write? Could it be we writers were all constantly looking for a place to belong?

My gaze roamed the room and saw intense concentration on the faces. Like all budding writers, these students were struggling to express their private thoughts, images, and notions to others via the written word, perhaps in this case recapturing a lost sense of home in the process.

I forgot the dingy surroundings and ignored the loud announcements. Instead, I allowed myself to share the joys of writing with this lively group of street people, whose expressions clearly indicated they'd left the grim outside world behind, if only for a few moments.

SHAWN WONG

ON TEACHING A WORKSHOP
FOR VETERANS

In the early '70s when I first started teaching, young Vietnam veterans were just starting to come back to college and were enrolling in my English classes. We were the same age—midtwenties. I wasn't drafted because I had a high lottery number. When they came back, I wanted to know their stories, particularly the story of the Asian American soldier sent to fight an Asian war. I interviewed and recorded the oral histories of many veterans, and though we were peers, I always felt that there was a huge gulf between us. I stayed in college, and they left. I could tell then that the person who came home wasn't the same person who'd gone to Vietnam.

In the summer of 2014, I was teaching a storytelling workshop in Walla Walla to fifteen Vietnam veterans as part of The Red Badge Project, cofounded by actor and Seattle resident Tom Skerritt and retired Army captain Evan Bailey, a veteran of both the Iraq and Afghanistan wars. For the previous two years, we had been teaching storytelling workshops at Joint Base Lewis-McChord in the Warrior Transition Battalion, along with instructors Warren Etheredge, Brian McDonald from TheFilmSchool in Seattle, and retired Navy combat photographer and former Clinton White House photographer and videographer Johnny Bivera. Skerritt had called all of us because he had read that the numbers of soldiers and veterans committing suicide was higher than the number dying in combat in Iraq or Afghanistan. One cause seemed to be the inability to articulate their stories while struggling with post-traumatic stress disorder (PTSD). Skerritt put together a team of storytellers.

In that first class two years ago, none of my students would make eye contact with me the first day of class. They looked down at their laptop screens or mobile phones or just at their desks. Two brought large German shepherds, anxiety service dogs. When I entered the classroom that first day, one of the dogs came bounding up to me, leapt up and placed his front paws on my shoulders, and backed me up against the wall, face-to-face. I found out later that these service dogs were trained to react this way or lean their weight against you when they sensed your elevated anxiety. I was anxious, and perhaps more so with a 160-pound German shepherd in my face. I had been told that some of my students might have paranoid schizophrenia, delusions, and/or PTSD. Many would be recuperating from surgery, managing pain, and most were angry. Loud noises made them grip the edges of their desks. My job was to teach them how to tell a story.

Skerritt brought an excerpt from the screenplay for the movie *Sideways*, for the students to read and act out. I had my doubts. But the script was a great icebreaker. Everyone laughed at the obviously flawed performances and at men having to play female roles.

Skerritt deftly directed each scene while soldiers dressed in camouflage acted out drinking Pinot Noir and talking about relationship strategies. By the third day, the soldiers were making eye contact, and one left her anxiety dog at home. By the fifth day, another soldier arranged a picnic lunch for everyone. Stories emerged not about combat or being in the Army, but about family, growing up, friendship, and the next life, after the Army.

That was how it started in 2012. We structured our classes to run for three hours a day for three weeks, then start a new class. What we didn't plan for was that, along with new students, the soldiers who had completed the course would sign up for the class again—and again, and again, and so on until they were discharged from the Army. One soldier who took the class five times said that the class saved his life. Many said it was better than therapy—it was therapeutic but not therapy. Evan Bailey explained our concept this way: one teacher explains why we need to tell stories, the next teacher tells us how, and finally, the last teacher makes us write it down. I'm the last one.

As a professor at the University of Washington, a public institution, it's essential that part of my job is to be a *public* scholar and to engage the community in a conversation about who we are. After forty-two years of teaching (thirty at the University of Washington), it was time for me to get out of the classroom and go on the road to find students who have something to say. They're not always going to come to me.

Back in Walla Walla, I realized I was facing essentially the same veterans I'd had in my class forty years ago. Those men were all older now, all of us in our sixties. I asked the vets in front of me to write a description from memory of any photograph that they were in. One of them wrote a description of his platoon in Vietnam sitting at their base drinking coffee—the relaxed moment between combat missions. I didn't ask him why he chose that photo, but I could tell there was a story. I wanted to get to the edge of the story, but not to the story itself. Let's just look at it as if it were a photo. Eventually, we'll get to tell *that* story.

BRUCE RUTLEDGE

Publisher, Chin Music Press

BRINGING MORE LITERATURE IN TRANSLATION TO AMERICA

My wife, Yuko Enomoto, and I lived in Japan for many years. We founded the press to bring out more literature in translation for an American audience. Americans are pretty impoverished when it comes to translations. We noticed that the Japanese, for example, have a wealth of the world's literature translated into their language. So we set out to balance the scales a bit, even if it's just a few books a year. The press has grown organically to include all sorts of literature, but we've kept our focus on Asia as much as possible.

NOT JUST FOR RICH PEOPLE'S COFFEE TABLES

The affordable part is always the catch. I'm not interested in making seventy-five-dollar art books to sit on some lucky rich person's coffee table. We want students and people on tight budgets to be able to purchase something beautiful and engaging too.

FREE BOOKS FOR THE PEOPLE

Before we moved into Pike Place Market, we worked in Fremont. On some sunny days, we'd put a box of spare books by the Lenin statue with a "Free" sign, and we'd watch people dig through and take what they want. It was oddly reaffirming to see people examine the books and slip them into their backpacks, even though we were giving them away.

THE ONE BOOK BY A SEATTLEITE TO PUT IN THE HANDS OF A VISITOR

Pour Your Heart Into It by Howard Schultz. Just kidding. I would like to read *How I Betrayed My City and Sold the Sonics to a Bunch of Okies* by Howard Schultz, but it hasn't been published yet.

Raymond Carver's not a Seattle writer, but he's just down the road: his *Will You Please Be Quiet, Please?* is beautiful and unsettling. And it always seems to be raining.

SEATTLE WRITER WHO DESERVES MORE ATTENTION

Bill Porter. Again, I'm stretching geography. He lives in Port Townsend. But he has an astounding knowledge of China and a warm, humorous storytelling style.

BEST LITERARY PERFORMER

I enjoyed watching Daniel Handler alternately scare the crap out of and excite a bunch of little kids at a local bookstore, and then, a couple of years later, bring down the house at Benaroya Hall with Sherman Alexie emceeing. Sherman couldn't stop laughing.

BEST NEIGHBORHOOD TO SET A MURDER MYSTERY

I would like to see a murder mystery set in South Lake Union.

BEST NEIGHBORHOOD TO SET A SCIENCE-FICTION NOVEL

Pike Place Market, where aliens infiltrate the human population without so much as a glance from us.

NEIGHBORHOOD BOOKSTORE OF CHOICE

We live in Magnolia, so Magnolia's Bookstore is our neighborhood store. The last book we bought there was *Drums, Girls & Dangerous Pie* by Jordan Sonnenblick for my eleven-year-old son. He loved it.

I am sort of a nomad when it comes to bookstores. I don't shop at any one store but love to roam the aisles of all the stores. I'm also a small-time collector. The last book I bought was a first-edition hardback of the *The Elements of Style* by E. B. White and William Strunk Jr. at the Globe Bookstore in Pioneer Square. That place has some hidden gems.

BEST DAY JOB FOR A WRITER IN SEATTLE

Working at the Elliott Bay Book Company. Or Third Place in Ravenna. Or manning the Espresso Book Machine at Third Place Press in Lake Forest Park. Or running the Chin Music showroom in Pike Place Market.

JUDITH ROCHE

ON BUMBERSHOOT

By 1985, the literary arts component of Bumbershoot was emerging as an important part of the annual Seattle arts festival. Believing in the power of literature, Louise DiLenge, the contessa of One Reel, Bumbershoot's producing company, hired me to produce the literary-arts program. The vision was to make Bumbershoot not just about music, but a celebration of all the arts, with out-of-town headliners bringing in the crowds but deep roots in local arts and artists. We had some high-profile greats at our table: Joseph Brodsky, Amiri Baraka, Diane di Prima, Michael Ondaatje, Allen Ginsberg, Tom Robbins, James Dickey, Carlos Fuentes, Ernesto Cardenal, Denise Levertov, Robert Hass, Robert Pinsky, Robert Creeley, Billy Collins, Sherman Alexie, Andrei Codrescu, and many more. We had the famous and the infamous on our stages. For the infamous, there was the year the rock 'n' roll guys were perfect gentlemen in their hotel rooms, but the *poet* Ai tore a phone out of its socket and threw it at a hotel worker.

There were so many luminous moments in the readings they blur together in the corridors of memory. One that stands out, though, is Robin Blaser, that great Canadian poet. He came in 1998 to read from his collection *The Holy Forest*. He was in his seventies and somewhat frail by then, and chain-smoked the whole time, on- and offstage. Of course, smoking inside at Seattle Center buildings was forbidden even in 1998, but no one dared tell *him* that. He was elegant, with a thick shock of silver-white hair, handsome, and distinguished—a "poet-priest" with a most dignified demeanor. His poems got to the core of what it is to be human and to love. Blaser had said his project in life and poetry was "to keep duty and love alive," and as he read from *The Holy Forest*, his words embodied that. Blaser's "holy forest" incorporated variously the world of nature, the house he lived in, the garden, and the city, with the Greek notion of the *polis*—all of it holy. I don't think I was the only one in the Alki Room who wept at that reading and came away with deeper sense of how to live more fully in one's time.

But the heart of the literary program remained the Northwest's own literary community, which centered on Bumbershoot Bookfair.

The Bookfair was the four-day party where we all gathered, greeted old friends, met news ones, made deals, and instigated book contracts. Paul Hunter and Tom Parson started the Bookfair as part of Bumbershoot long before One Reel took over the festival. It was already a happening thing when One Reel became producer, and continued to be the beating heart of the lit community, supported by budget decisions at the top. It included Seattle presses and many Canadian presses, like Talonbooks, *Pacific Rim Review of Books,* and *Raddle Moon*, out of British Columbia. It also included Calyx, out of Oregon; *Poetry Flash,* from Berkeley; Graywolf Press, from Minneapolis; poet Charlie Potts, from Walla Walla; writer

Polly Buckingham, from StringTown, near Spokane; and many others. It was a true gathering of tribes, the tribes here being Cascadia's independent presses and writers.

With so many friends and soon-to-be friends in town for four days, we had to have a party. Several years before I actually worked for Bumbershoot, I started to have a Bumbershoot party at my house. Fifty, eighty, ninety or so people would show up at my (small) house after the last Saturday night reading, and it was always a raucous event. Being certainly a party girl, I loved it. However, after I started working the event—with months of preparation, days of load-in, and working eighteen hours a day during event days—it became way too much for me. The last time I hosted the party, I remember trying to go to bed at 2 a.m. (oh God, I had to be back on-grounds at 8 a.m. and work another fifteen-hour day) and hearing tribal drumming from my living room led by Don Wilson, Michael Hureaux Perez, Roberto Valenza, and other inveterate partiers. It was loud, certainly drunken, and showed no signs of stopping. I think I shouted, "Go home!" from my bed, but I probably wasn't even heard with all that drumming going on. The party had its own life, and I couldn't stop it. I simply couldn't do it anymore.

The next year there was a line item in my budget for an event called the Literary Soiree. The Soiree went on for years after, though probably not as raucously as the parties at my house, being at various restaurants and venues, including on-site at Seattle Center. But still, it was a gathering of the tribes and an important part of the festival for participants. In those days, we created a community, which is ephemeral. Things change, new vitality in a community arises, but we started something.

NICOLE HARDY

ON WHERE SHE WRITES

If you count talking about writing as writing, which I do, I often write at Oddfellows Cafe. On any given day, it can turn into a literary salon. The initial draw might be its proximity to the Elliott Bay Book Company and Richard Hugo House, but really it's the camaraderie, and the deviled eggs. At Oddfellows, Peter Mountford talked to me in very fast sentences about why early drafts of my memoir were failing. I took an impromptu lecture on nontraditional memoir with Elissa Washuta. Claire Dederer talked me off a precipitous ledge of resistance to the arc of a project struggling to make itself clear. Suzanne Morrison helped me through more than one writing-related existential crisis. And fellow Modern Love essayists Theo Nestor, Wilson Diehl, and I fell in love with one another's work. I could go on about the chance meetings, make an exhaustive list of the invaluable moments, but the point is this: one can't pop in for a cheese plate or glass of wine (or the eggs, the eggs, the eggs) without running into another writer or two or three, hunched over their laptops, or leaning into a conversation at one of the heavy

wooden tables, thirsty for (or drunk on) the encouragement, com-
miseration, or inspiration that's always at the ready.

I've seen dozens of authors read at the Elliott Bay Book Company,
but the day the store hosted Jane Hirshfield may have actually
changed my life. I don't buy into all the New Age airy-fairy hippie
bullshit that requires one to wear Birkenstocks and have fantasies
about community farms and flaxseed. But I swear on a soul-
cleansing pyre of burning Birkenstocks that Jane Hirshfield is, like,
some sort of priestess. She was reading from her newest collection,
her flowing hair backlit by the reading light, her face glowing with
poetic brilliance and Zen and newfound love—"it feels the same,"
she said, "when you're in your fifties." And in the transition from
one poem to another, she interpreted the recurring dream that had
sent me sleepwalking through my house for years. She made a metaphor that shot through me like a revelation. If we'd been cast in
a made-for-TV movie, there would've been a flash of lightning to
punctuate it. I didn't hear anything she said after that. I have no
idea what she wrote in the book she signed for me. Here's what I
do know: I never had the dream after that night. Never, ever. Not
even once. Now try to tell me that's not spooky.

One afternoon in the café at Elliott Bay, I looked up to see no less
than fifteen other Seattle writers—a large table having a workshop,
a bunch of singletons sucking down coffee, scribbling, reading, or
typing. "Look at this," I said to a friend at the large table as we both
scanned the room. Another woman, a stranger, said, "I often think
Seattle right now is what Paris was in the twenties."

PART 4

PERFORMING

KAREN FINNEYFROCK

ON POETRY AND PLATE-GLASS WINDOWS

The King Cat (with a *C*) was a '70s movie theater in the Denny Triangle that showed *Close Encounters of the Third Kind* as a first run. It lasted a decade, then reopened as the King Kat (with a *K*), a rock venue where Nirvana played. Another decade and that venue went under, so the site briefly hosted a megachurch, and then took one last retro gasp as a combination rock club/movie theater. Last year it was demolished for new corporate headquarters. So there's the direction of Seattle progress. Movie theater. Rock club. Megachurch. Corporate HQ.

In 2001, the King Kat rock venue had a huge hall, capacity of eighteen hundred, in a stout, boxy cement building with a lobby enclosed on three sides by glass. It was one of those venues always eulogized by the nostalgic punk at the party. One time, he saw Jello Biafra there. Another time, he saw the Melvins. He'll tell you about it by the backyard fire pit while the light casts his shadow onto the new condos going up next door.

I first encountered the King Kat while on the committee to produce the National Poetry Slam. A weeklong tournament for spoken-word artists hosted in a different city every year, NPS is a diametrically imagined event. It is both the premier competition for poetry slam (a performance poetry contest popular around the world) and a one-off festival produced by a scrappy band of volunteers more accustomed to throwing shows in basements than high-capacity concert halls. This tension creates an event that is professional, capable of becoming a career-maker for the poets who win, and prone to the amateur missteps of volunteer staff. Imagine March Madness presented by your local community theater.

My job, despite being the newest transplant to Seattle on the committee, was managing venues. Specifically, I had to call renowned Seattle rock clubs and dive bars like the Crocodile and the Central Saloon and convince them that crowds would pack into their clubs to stand, drink, and listen to poetry. This suggestion elicited the common response "Did you say *poetry*?"

There was no need to convince the King Kat. We just had to pay the fee, sign the contract, and provide proof of insurance. It was slated to present a semifinal team bout and individual finals, some of the biggest shows in the festival. The venue manager was your standard Seattle rock-club guy. Buddy Holly glasses, black rock T-shirt, wallet chain, at least one tattoo sleeve, unfazed by a moon landing when he's sober, but ready to riot over an a poorly twisted garnish when he's not.

After two nights of preliminary bouts, Nationals were rolling along like civilization's first wheel. It was a Friday evening in August around eight. A heavy breeze sent the smell of sea air all the way up Blanchard, and there was a chalky glow of evening light reflecting off the glass walls of the King Kat lobby. Inside the theater, our show was under way. Since it was one of four concurrent semifinal bouts happening around the city, I sat in the lobby with my radio waiting for the calls to come in.

"This is Sit & Spin. Our show just started."
"The bout is under way at the Crocodile."
"Semifinal in progress at Dutch Ned's."

Months of stressy e-mails and panicked phone calls would be over by the end of the night. I sighed with near freedom and overexhaustion. There was only one more show to launch, individual finals, the late event at the King Kat and a festival high point. All the audience members from the other three venues would be walking, driving, or busing to our venue to see it. The outcome would name the National Poetry Slam Champion of the year.

In the lobby, a steady flow of volunteers buzzed around, folding T-shirts on the merch table, selling tickets to the early and late shows. The atmosphere was so calm I decided to step out into the alley with some friends, and one offered me his joint. I wasn't a huge pot smoker, but the festival atmosphere made me a little reckless. I was twenty-eight and blowing off steam from a hard week of long days. I came back into the venue mildly stoned, and slipped inside the theater to hear a few poems.

The bout was hot. I remember a group piece about consumerism, in which poets turned the word "Wal-Mart" into a droning chant. You know how you say a word enough times and it loses meaning?

The poets changed "Wal-Mart" from profane to holy to nonsensical by repeating it for three minutes straight. It was spellbinding. The audience erupted after that piece and many others. Maybe that's why I didn't hear what was going on in the lobby.

When I left the theater again and turned my radio back on, everything was wrong. I caught the tail end of someone calling for the festival directors. I caught the word "injury." A volunteer ran past me with an ice pack. Two workmen followed with a comically large piece of plywood. Someone with an industrial broom was sweeping glass into a pile on the carpet, and the sea-smelling night air blew through my hair. Then the venue manager was in front of me.

"I'm pulling the show," he said. "Your audience is out of control. Show me your event insurance or I'm yanking the mics."

It took frantic minutes to coax the story out of him. Apparently, an audience member meant to exit through one of the glass double doors to go outside and smoke a cigarette. Instead, he walked into a glass wall with his face. Venue Guy delivered the news with implication: *Your poetry audience is OUT OF CONTROL! Everyone here is WASTED! This is ten times crazier than when RANCID was here.*

Around this time, I became extremely self-conscious about being stoned. I coaxed Venue Guy into the office and stalled until the festival directors, Bob Redmond and Allison Durazzi, showed up wearing nervous smiles. They exchanged handshakes and insurance riders and sent me to hang out with the injured guy and wait for the ambulance. Allison said, "See if he seems, you know, *impaired*." Maybe the most difficult job to assign someone who is "impaired" is to determine if a stranger is also impaired. Besides hair long enough for a horsetail, the guy who walked into the wall

displayed no obvious signs of intoxication. He was also miracu-
lously unhurt, with only a small cut on the bridge of his nose. He
seemed almost apologetic about the whole thing.

Inside the office, the festival directors convinced Venue Guy that
the scene would get ugly if he stopped the show, and they agreed
to work out insurance details in the morning. The ambulance came
and went, the pile of shards disappeared from the carpet, and the
glass wall was replaced with a tidy slab of plywood while the four
hundred audience members inside the theater enjoyed the final
minutes of the show unaware. The situation was already coalesc-
ing into an anecdote for the festival postmortem, already fading
into Nationals lore. And then the second person walked into a
glass wall.

In a lobby filled with people who were incapable of conversation that did not involve the words "glass wall," a volunteer who
was busy folding T-shirts said, "I'm going to grab some more shirts
from the van." Then he turned and walked through a window.

I thought Venue Guy was going to peel off his tattoos like a wet
suit and shred all the grease from his pompadour. The infamous
King Kat, where the Melvins and Crash Worship played, was being
reduced to literal shards by a bunch of performance poets. His brain
must have been overwhelmed with conspiracy theories. *Maybe we
were all on a new club drug popular only in the poetry scene.* But the
T-shirt volunteer had been working on the show for hours, and his
dinner had consisted of cold pizza and warm soda, not horse tran-
quilizers and bourbon.

When asked what happened, the volunteer's primary response
was embarrassment. He couldn't believe it had happened either.

The most jarring difference between the two cases was that the second guy didn't even get a cut on his nose. It was like an opening scene in a superhero movie, where the lead doesn't yet know he's invincible but emerges from a bomb blast feeling a tad chilly. I played an unwitting extra, mumbling to the camera, "That guy's got a tough forehead."

Chaos erupted again. Everyone seemed to be running somewhere to get something that had to be gotten immediately. The merch table became a makeshift first-aid station. People keep floating curiously closer to the remains of the wall while other people yelled, "Get back." Glass debris was spread around the lobby entrance, and the barrier between inside and outside vanished as people reported the events through the breach to the crowd gathering outside.

That's when the second set of radio calls came in.

"Show just wrapped at the Crocodile. Four hundred people are headed up the hill."

"We're packing up at Sit & Spin. You should get our crowd any minute."

"Bout is over at Dutch Ned's. A mob is walking your way."

In my memory, the audience members are zombies, converging on us from all sides, so long-dead on poetry their only desire is not for brains but to fling themselves bodily through plate glass. They moaned and dragged their way out of the theater by the hundreds, mumbling about bathrooms and cigarettes. From outside the building, an endless stream of pale faces stumbled out of the darkness toward the lobby, shambling in the direction of the remaining glass windows, prepared to gain entry with their unbreakable, undead faces.

I mustered the remaining volunteers like ragtag survivors, grouping them around me for a rousing speech. "See those glass walls?" I said to my frightened, unpaid staff. "Pick one and don't let anyone walk through it."

The next sixty minutes were a blur. The directors didn't try to talk calmly with Venue Guy this time. They looked at the new pile of glass on the carpet and said, "We'll get the checkbook." More giant brooms appeared from the janitorial closet, and more plywood came from somewhere. Patrons approaching the venue from the street saw volunteers in matching T-shirts strung between the walls of the lobby like paper dolls and heard workmen screwing a barricade onto the building.

In the decade since, theories have arisen. Did the strange quality of the August evening light turn the walls invisible? Had the windows been recently cleaned, causing a pileup of bird carcasses that had been swept away before we arrived? Or was it just the old mystery of coincidence, another visit from the unexplainable, unpredictable element of chance?

More than twelve hundred people were ferried safely past those glass walls and into the once-movie-hall-turned-rock-venue that, for one night, presented poetry. They were that nearly mythical audience of word lovers in a world dominated by cellulose and amps. In the dark theater, the poems swept up the shards, hung shiny new plates of glass, revived our rotting corpses, and made the movies play again.

FRANCES McCUE

ON TOM ROBBINS AND HIS BODYGUARDS

My job was to meet Tom Robbins in the alley behind the Tower Records in the U District in Seattle. This was in 1987, or maybe it was early in 1988.

"Why the alley?" I asked. "Why not in the lobby of the bookstore across the street or something?"

"That's what he wants," Colleen McElroy said. She looked fiercely at me. Back then, the MFA program at the University of Washington was newly formed. (It used to be an MA degree, and Colleen had been the one to get the *F* added to it.) Colleen was a well-known poet and the program's director. She was also the faculty advisor for the Watermark Reading Series. I was a student volunteer, and we Watermark people had decided to invite Tom Robbins to give a reading on campus.

"So I bring him from there over to Kane Hall?"

Colleen looked at me. "Yes, and you be sure that he isn't late." She lowered her eyebrows.

Colleen bossed me around. Partly because I was the youngest person in the MFA program and partly because I have an instinct to both rebel and attach, I took to her. I was a girl with a mouth and some smarts, and what smarts I didn't have, I used my mouth to make up for. I was pretty ambitious. I wanted to get this whole literary business right. Later, I figured out that Colleen had some of the same traits—she too had been an only child from her mother's first failed marriage, and she had also been a bookish, mouthy kid who got out of the place where she began and headed west.

So on the appointed night, I walked over to Forty-Third, one of the side streets off of University Way. I headed up behind the big Tower Records. (Big 5 Sporting Goods is there now.) The alley was filthier then—crowded with Dumpsters and metal trash cans. It was early evening, and the day's refuse had steamed and settled. The place stunk. I came along the trench of broken pavement, and when I looked up, I saw a little man standing between two bigger guys. They looked down the alley at me.

That's the first thing about Tom Robbins. He's smaller than you think he'll be. He has this impish crooked grin and some prickly blond hair, and he's light and small. But the other guys weren't. They were big, thick guys.

"Hey," Tom said.

"Hi," I said, and introduced myself.

"This is Bob," Tom said. He pointed to the man with a little beard scruff. "And this is Bob," he added, pointing to the other one.

"Hi." I was staring at the three of them: Tom in the middle with these guys bookending him. I nodded to the two men. "You guys are both named Bob?"

"Yes, they are," said Robbins. "I'm Tom. These are Bobs."

I reached out and shook Tom's hand. The Bobs flinched a little. One leaned in, over our handshake.

"They are my bodyguards," Tom said, flicking his thumbs in either direction.

The Bobs had bulges in the chests of their overcoats.

"Guns? Do they have guns?"

"Of course they have guns," Tom said. "Listen, I was at Berkeley recently, and some woman threw a bottle at me right out of the audience. It was crazy."

Maybe it was *Jitterbug Perfume* or *Even Cowgirls Get the Blues* that had ticked them off. Whatever it was, things didn't go over well at Berkeley for the feminist contingent. This was confusing for me. Tom Robbins, the radical novelist whom the radical feminists didn't like. Back then, I thought radical was radical. I didn't know that different parts of radical might not take to each other.

"Okay," I said. What did I know? I had a lot to learn. I was maybe twenty-four years old and didn't have the slightest idea about how cool Tom Robbins was or how famous or what was necessary for a writer of that stature. Bodyguards? Okay then.

I walked with Tom and his Bobs over to the Roethke Auditorium at Kane Hall. Amazing, as I think of it now, how many world-class writers have read in that space: Adrienne Rich, Seamus Heaney, John Berryman, Elizabeth Bishop, Richard Hugo—Nobel laureates, Pulitzer Prize and National Book Award winners, you name it.

It's one of Seattle's longest-lasting literary crossroads, and it's set right on Red Square in a bunker-like structure next to the ventilation tower from the parking garage. Thousands of kids a day come in and out of Kane Hall for big lecture classes. I once watched Raymond Carver and Tess Gallagher make their way up the aisles in that space, Tess flicking back her long hair, and Ray in a long overcoat, a big man, looking for a seat at some reading I now can't remember.

When Tom and the Bobs and I got to Kane Hall, we went into a room behind the auditorium.

I said, "I saved some seats for Bob and Bob—"

"No, Bob and Bob will be onstage with me," Tom said.

"But I have seats in the front row for them—"

Tom turned and snapped, "How the *fuck* will they shoot anyone if they are sitting in the front row?"

I didn't have an answer for that. This was before Public Enemy taught us all about having an aggressive presence onstage.

"Oh wow," I said. "Oh."

I think I went to Colleen and told her what was going on. I can't remember whether she asked the Bobs to take a seat or what, but the auditorium was full that night. Tom read his wild work, and people cheered, and nobody threw a bottle, and the Bobs didn't have to open fire. No one got hurt. Afterward, we went to China Harbor, that big black-glassed, impossible-to-see-in restaurant on Lake Union, where I sat next to Tom's wife, Alexa. She's a clairvoyant. When I met her, I realized people really can be clairvoyants. She was sensible and sweet—not at all flaky.

The world, then, seemed full of possibility. At dinner, I made jokes about the "Bobs bobbing to shore" from La Conner, the town along the sea sluices up north where Tom and Alexa lived. Colleen laughed, and Tom smirked, not in bad way. In the parking lot, I said good-bye to Alexa, and she gave me a little hug while Tom leaned in and said, "Good job." The Bobs smiled and waved, and pulled their overcoats shut. The four of them bundled into a car, and from where I stood, I could see them laughing all the way out onto Westlake Avenue, roaring on to their next adventure.

CHARLES R. CROSS

ON STEVEN "JESSE" BERNSTEIN

As a book lover, an editor, and an author in Seattle, I have seen many memorable readings over the years. Those I've heard have included the infamous, the obscure, and, occasionally, the true legend. Margaret Atwood read poetry to me on a sofa in a Madison Park home. Allen Ginsberg hit on me over a pot of tea. I once took a limo to Sea-Tac with Tom Wolfe; when his flight was delayed, I spent five hours in an airport lounge listening to his tales of Hunter S. Thompson and Ken Kesey. I met Kesey himself a few years later and held his hat for him during a reading. I also met Thompson, but that encounter involved enough illegality that little should be spoken of it, even today. All of that happened to me while I was in college; the stories since are even juicier.

As the author of nine books, I have also had some of my own memorable readings. My upcoming memoir starts off with a story about my then-five-year-old raising his hand to ask a question at a reading I gave at Elliott Bay a few years back. I've written biographies of musicians Jimi Hendrix and Kurt Cobain, and both have attracted conspiracy theorists who have occasionally interrupted my readings. If having stalkers sounds glamorous, it's not, though having a screaming attendee dragged away from a bookstore by police does tend make a reading memorable for all involved.

When it comes to Seattle book readings where drama, tension, and actual bloodshed were involved, none I've ever given or witnessed tops a poetry reading in Pioneer Square at the Graven Image Gallery in the '80s. It involved a switchblade, a penis, blood, fecal matter, perhaps a live mouse, many threats to the audience, and some to the poet. It also was attended by a handful of people (including myself) who would soon play a role in the Seattle music scene that took the world by storm in the early '90s.

The poet was Steven "Jesse" Bernstein, who at the time was just gaining a reputation in Seattle. He would later release an album on Sub Pop, open up for grunge bands (including Nirvana), and be called the "Godfather of Grunge" by the British paper the *Independent*. I knew Jesse and had attended a number of his readings. He also occasionally wrote for the magazine I edited, the *Rocket*. (We once had him interview William S. Burroughs for us.) A month or so before this most memorable reading, I was sitting in a bar with Jesse when an angry paramour of his threw a brick at the plate-glass window we were sitting behind. That was one of two times I was near Jesse when I was showered with glass (the other was a fight at a punk rock club). Jesse not only attracted drama, but he often created it.

The Graven Image reading was organized by Larry Reid. I remember it as a summer night, with three dozen or so people in the crowd. Jesse's Bukowski-esque poetry did not appeal to everyone, and after a few poems, the crowd began to heckle him. (I think a punk rock band was to follow his reading, but many details, beyond what I am about to disclose, are hazy to me.) Jesse told the hecklers to "fuck off." The hecklers told him to "fuck off." A few people left. Then Jesse pulled a long object out of his pocket, hit a button, and, like in a '50s movie, a switchblade unfolded. He pointed it at the crowd but soon had a better idea it seemed. He unzipped his fly, pulled his penis out, and put the switchblade at the base.

"If anyone else leaves, I'm going to cut my cock off," he said in his dry monotone.

It did not appear to be an act. The knife was sharp enough that as he pressed it against the base of his penis, a little blood came out.

A man in the front row dramatically stood up and walked out. Jesse looked at him, and then looked at the knife against his penis, and paused.

There is an adage of playwriting that if the writer shows you a gun onstage, it will be fired. If a similar adage could be applied to punk-rock poetry readings, it should be "Poets should not put a knife against their penis and threaten to cut it off, unless they are going to."

Another man stood up and left. The crowd that remained began to chant, "Cut it off!"

Jesse quickly pivoted. He screamed, "I'm going to cut off the penis of the next person who leaves!" A woman got up and left. Jesse paused again, but this time only for a moment. "I'm going to *stab* the next person who leaves, in the heart."

That worked. No one else left.

After a few more poems, Jesse put the still-unfolded switchblade in his pocket, and while holding his poetry chapbook in one hand, he started to finger his butt rhythmically. This was actually harder to watch than the switchblade against his dick.

Someone cried out, "Gross!" Jesse took his hand out of his ass, grabbed the switchblade again, and threatened the crowd.

There was a tiny bit of fecal matter on his finger, and by then, the room had a "bathroomy" smell to it. I so wanted to leave, but I was as afraid of Jesse's poop-specked hand as I was of his switchblade.

I remembered that speck of brown when I began researching Kurt Cobain's life, and discovered that Kurt had seen at least one of Jesse's early readings and perhaps was at this one. Kurt was a complete unknown then; a skinny blond kid in the audience wouldn't have stood out. Kurt shared some of Jesse's same obsessions, and the name of his first band, the first version of Nirvana, was Fecal Matter. My guess is Kurt saw Jesse a couple of years later, but it is impossible to know, and a number of the people in the crowd were from the same crew of musicians and artists that hung out at the nearby Metropolis.

I saw many of Jesse's readings during that era, and at another he urinated on a heckling attendee. The reason I said that "perhaps" a live mouse was involved in the Graven Image reading is because I can't honestly remember if it was there that Jesse had his mouse. I do know for certain that at a couple of readings Jesse pulled out his pet mouse, Blinky, and read with Blinky in his mouth. I witnessed it, but I can't definitively say when it happened. It says a lot about how dominant the switchblade/penis action was in my memory that it could overshadow a writer reading with a live animal in his mouth. It also may be that the mutilation of a penis with a switchblade scares me more than a rodent. (Jesse always licked the mouse before sticking him in his mouth, and I found that more disturbing than watching Blinky's tail flop in and out.) When Jesse read with the mouse in his mouth, he had to mumble, so the poetry itself was less effective as poetry even as it remained incredible performance art.

I've seen plenty of performance art over the years, which sometimes is masked as literature. Larry Reid once brought Karen Finley's infamous "yam jam" show to Seattle. That was a show that involved Finley, her butt, and a can of yams. (You do the math.) That kind of event seemed typical of New York, where Finley was from. But "yam jam" could happen anywhere.

Jesse's switchblade/penis/mouse act was homegrown, it seemed to me, and it felt purely Seattle, if only because it was held before a very small audience in what at the time was a derelict and run-down part of town. The linkage between grunge and early Seattle punk-rock poetry readings is important to note. "Smells Like Teen Spirit" was first played live (a few years later) at a venue just two blocks from that Graven Image poetry reading, but both artistic creations were off-center enough to be interesting. That's what Jesse Bernstein shared with the other acts on Sub Pop: they were all just a bit fucked-up, and it was that very fucked-up-ness that made them interesting. Kurt Cobain's genius was making fucked-up lyrics and music palatable and catchy.

Jesse Bernstein's switchblade reading ended without major mayhem, but there was a spot of blood on his pants. Visual memory is trickier than other senses, because traumatic real-life events often feel like dreams even years later. Other senses are more accurate, and the "bathroomy" smell of the tiny gallery on that hot day is still seared in my memory. In a way, it was a failed reading, as the poetry was lost to the drama, but it was one night I'll never forget.

I went on to write about Northwest music for many outlets, and eventually become an author. Kurt Cobain, who is the subject of my 2001 book *Heavier Than Heaven*, went on to create a musical revolution that would change culture. Larry Reid went on to run Center on Contemporary Art for years and book Nirvana there, and now is in charge of the Fantagraphics Bookstore in Georgetown.

Jesse Bernstein suffered with depression, addiction, and bipolar illness. He died in 1991—almost at the moment the entire world began to notice Seattle's music culture. Jesse went out in a dramatic suicide that also involved a knife: he stabbed himself to death near Neah Bay.

In the years since his death, Jesse's poetry has gained new readers and a bit of literary respect. Oliver Stone used one of Jesse's recordings in *Natural Born Killers*. A 2010 documentary on Jesse, *I Am Secretly an Important Man*, contains footage of Jesse reading with Blinky in his mouth. It is something to watch.

The switchblade/penis reading was not filmed, as far as I know. It exists only in the memory of the few who were there, and some of them are dead. But like most great Seattle stories, it is so weird, so strange, and so unique that you simply couldn't make it up. You had to be there.

I never heard what happened to Blinky.

WILLIE FITZGERALD
AND TARA ATKINSON

Two of the Founders of the APRIL Festival

HOW IT ALL GOT STARTED

Willie Fitzgerald: APRIL started as an offshoot of Pilot Books, a wonderful clubhouse-like bookstore that sold only small-press titles. Our friend Summer Robinson ran the place, and that's where the founders APRIL met (that'd be Summer, Tara Atkinson, and myself) and where a lot of the burgeoning Seattle writing community used to hang out. APRIL started as SPF (Small Press Festival), and it was an extension of Pilot Books' regular in-store readings. After Pilot went out of business in May 2011, we decided to keep the spirit of the place alive in a series of events. We changed the name to APRIL (Authors, Publishers & Readers of Independent Literature) and tried to cram a year's worth of great literary events into a single week.

Tara Atkinson: Pilot was really like one shared living room for a group of young writers, a space where we could share our lives and writing without being roommates and having to talk about who was going to clean the bathtub. We'd stick around after pretty much every reading to hang out. Once, I applied a temporary tattoo to someone's chest with a can of PBR. During the day, Pilot was a great, quiet place to write. You would face a shelf full of very beautiful books when you sat on the comfy couch; it was a very friendly and attractive place where there was really no reason for anyone who wasn't a book lover to show up. Writing in a library or a coffee shop really isn't the same. There was also this near-constant buzz of tattoo needles from the tattoo place across the hall that resonated a kind of alt-ness.

Willie Fitzgerald: So that was sort of the primordial soup from which APRIL emerged. (APRIL's not the only Pilot descendent, either: Matt Nelson, one of the founders of Mellow Pages Library & Reading Room in Brooklyn, was a Pilot regular. Pilot Books had that sort of effect on people.) Anyway, Summer left shortly after we changed our name to APRIL. Kellen Braddock joined right around when Summer was leaving. Frances Chiem joined APRIL the next year, and Kenny Coble the year after that.

READING AND DANCING

Tara Atkinson: Last year, it was raining when I left my house to set up for our opening party at Chop Suey, and I had this foil dragon balloon with raindrops clinging to it, so it was a very melancholy but poetic trip. When I walked into this big, empty event venue with a foil dragon and a bunch of warm lights, where the bartender was slicing lemons, all of the gray outside was eclipsed by the anticipation of a big party. There's a big window in Chop Suey's side room with a view of the street, and as door time drew closer, it got dark outside and I could see people lining up. That reading featured Maged Zaher, Ed Skoog, and Jac Jemc. Maged and Ed are both Seattle poets with different styles and even more different personalities onstage. Maged is a very animated reader, but a lot of his poems are about romantic failures, sort of self-deprecating. He lives half the year in Egypt, and he read several poems by Egyptian poets, which he had translated. Then Ed read. He has a sort of stentorian majesty. His poems are more about memory and landscape. Then Jac Jemc, who was visiting from Chicago, read a sort of surreal/fabulist, very serious story. Then a band played, and we danced. The whole night made me really feel the range of possibilities that exists for writing.

I remember lots of other readings I've been to in Seattle for their own reasons. A reading APRIL hosted at Blindfold Gallery with Shin Yu Pai and Zubair Ahmed was totally packed; that made me feel pretty excited (also nervous that I would cough). When I talked to Shin Yu Pai after, she mentioned how many Asian Americans she could see in the audience and how great that was to see. Washington Ensemble Theatre's Six Pack Series always has a really loud and animated crowd and theatrical hosts, which makes literature feel really fun. Sherman Alexie at the *Stranger*'s Verse Chapter Verse (which has a band, followed by a reading, followed by an interview, followed by the band again) reminded me that there are writers who can get "big" but still support independent publishers and speak up about things like criticism in poetry—I guess I mean not "sell out," which sounds cliché, but there really are so many writers out there whose advice is all about elevator pitches and publicity. It feels very Seattle to me that our most famous author would be indie-minded and opinionated. I've loved house-party readings, where everyone was chummy and I felt lots of goodwill and community, which is important, because writing is often so lonely. And I've been to more serious "big" readings with established writers, like Hugo's Literary Series at Hugo House, which stoked my ambition to be taken seriously too.

A POET, A PLAYWRIGHT, A NOVELIST, AND A DRAG QUEEN

Willie Fitzgerald: Every year, we have a drag queen read as part of our competitive storytelling event, *A Poet, a Playwright, a Novelist, and a Drag Queen*. Jackie Hell, one of our favorite drag queens, won second place in the first-ever competition. She told a story about seducing a man for a new refrigerator, and repeatedly employed the phrase "a strappy Lane Bryant number." We invited her back to our next year's launch party to give the festival a "dedication," and she sang a song about stabbing people and being a witch, I think. It was amazing. I remember seeing Rebecca Brown—she was going to read right after Jackie was done—gazing openmouthed at this knife-wielding lady in runny pancake makeup. It was like she'd seen a religious idol or a phantasmal horror.

BAR CRAWLS AND FLASH MOBS

Willie Fitzgerald: At the first APRIL, in 2012, we did a literary bar crawl that accumulated a much-bigger crowd than we'd anticipated along the way. We were traveling all together in a pack from one place to another and kept picking up more people. We basically flash-mobbed a karaoke night at the Crescent. Poet Sarah Galvin was completely the right person to hold her own against the hecklers there. At one point, she yelled back, "Shut up or buy me a drink!" Despite that, some of the karaokers joined us. The last stop was supposed to be in my brother Aidan's apartment, but there were one hundred people with us by then, so we snuck into the building's parking garage. The landlady heard us, and my brother expertly intercepted her and kept us from getting caught. Then Ed Skoog read a poem he'd written just for that occasion, while standing in front a giant, forlorn water heater that someone had spray-painted with the word "Drama." He patted it and said it was his artificial heart.

THE ONE BOOK BY A SEATTLEITE TO PUT IN THE HANDS OF A VISITOR

Tara Atkinson: Maged Zaher's *Thank You for the Window Office*. Cities don't really have two sides, but my experience living here does, more or less. One is the "art" world where most of my social interactions take place, and the other is the "business" world that I see around me in office buildings and demolition sites and cranes and Microsoft buses and lanyards and commuter traffic. Maged writes about both of those Seattle worlds, so I'd want a visitor to have the complete and condensed portrait of Seattle that he captures.

SEATTLE WRITER WHO DESERVES MORE ATTENTION

Willie Fitzgerald: Everyone should read something by Matthew Simmons, Rebecca Brown, Shin Yu Pai, Ed Skoog, Sarah Galvin, Piper Daniels, Maged Zaher, Stacey Levine—the list could really go on. I love Bill Carty's work. Ditto for Don Mee Choi, Peter Mountford, and Richard Chiem. Ask an impossible question, get a long-winded answer.

BEST NEIGHBORHOOD TO SET A MURDER MYSTERY

Willie Fitzgerald: I could see a *Twin Peaks*-ian murder happening in Wallingford, with its moss-bedecked gutters and expertly manicured gardens. Also, my brother used to live in a house that was owned by cultists. There's room for an *Inspector Morse*-style murder mystery there, though the lead detective probably would never leave his rain pants.

BEST NEIGHBORHOOD TO SET A SCIENCE-FICTION NOVEL

Willie Fitzgerald: I'd leave the bland utopian aesthetic of Capitol Hill and head down to Georgetown, with its lots full of rusted-out truck chassis and its giant cowboy-boot sculpture. I don't know what kind of future that'd be, exactly, but it'd probably be pretty cool.

NEIGHBORHOOD BOOKSTORE OF CHOICE

Tara Atkinson: Elliott Bay is usually my go-to, but the library is closer. I like to go on these library binges where I pick one title that I want and schedule it to be delivered to the branch closest to me, and then I use the library's "search the shelf" function and pick out ten books like it, and I walk home looking like a cartoon nerd or something. My last binge was all about trying to finish a personal essay I'm working on. I brought home Tin House's *The Writer's Notebook,* which is a collection of craft essays from its summer workshop; John D'Agata's giant essay anthology *The Lost Origins of the Essay*; and probably about six other books. And I always rush to finish them before they're due back. It's very motivating!

Willie Fitzgerald: It's not in my neighborhood, but we're so, so lucky to have Open Books in town. That place is as important to Seattle as the Space Needle, as far as I'm concerned. I think the last thing I bought there was Homage to the *Lame Wolf by Vasko Popa,* or else it was something by James Tate.

BEST DAY JOB FOR A WRITER IN SEATTLE

Tara Atkinson: If APRIL were one person with a shared job history, she would have worked as a proofreader, copywriter, produce dispatcher, nanny, short-order cook, bookseller, journalist, teacher, communications specialist, receptionist, housepainter, and handyman. None of these jobs are particularly good for writing (the act), but they're good for the writer (the actor), because without them there'd be nothing to procrastinate with, and the whole world would probably fall in on itself.

REBECCA BROWN
ON JACK STRAW AND HUGO HOUSE

Red and Black was a not-for-profit bookstore collective that had been around for decades. In the late '90s, it was going bust, so I organized a bunch of theme readings as fund-raisers. Our first reading was in February, near Valentine's Day, so we made it The Heart Reading, and people read or performed ridiculous stories about romance or medicine or both, and a couple of women dressed up in skimpy cocktail aprons over their sensible clothes and passed around cut-up bits of Pop-Tarts with toothpicks in them, like appetizers, because "tart" rhymes with "heart" and can also mean "a naughty lady." My friend Donna dressed up in doctor drag and brought a big medical specimen jar filled with blood-red food-colored water and a hunk of mozzarella so it looked like a severed heart, and I read a piece called "Have a Heart" about eating one. Another one of the themes later on had something to do with the body as machine, and I invited my next-door neighbor, the writer Jesse Minkert, who got dialysis, to read about being a body and a machine, and his wife, Joan Rabinowitz, said it was one of Jesse's best readings ever and she wanted to start a program for writers at Jack Straw Cultural Center and did I want to do it? Sure, I said, I'd love to come up with an alternative way for writers to get their work out.

By that time—it was 1997, and I'd first moved to Seattle in the early '80s—I'd been turned down for every single grant I'd ever applied for in Seattle, King County, Washington State, etc., and I was bitter about the whole concept of having to predict and describe to committees of arts funders what my creative work would be and how it would reach new audiences and have a positive effect on our society. So, writers applying for the Jack Straw Writers Program— which would provide a reading venue and series, and a quality sound recording of their work—would not have to go through the rigamarole of that kind of application; they'd just submit their work and be selected on its merits. The first year, we got a huge pile of applications. I selected fourteen writers, among them Donna Miscolta, Riz Rollins, Amy Halloran, Joan Fiset, John McFarland, Kate Berne Miller, George Wolfe, and Noel Franklin, some whose work or style I recognized when reading the applications, others completely new to me. Graphic artist Aldo Chan, who later walked me down the aisle when Chris and I had our commitment ceremony, designed a chapbook for the first reading, which took place at the Jack Straw studio. Chris made a huge celebratory frosted sheet cake, and we all ate like kids and got giddy on sugar and happiness. The Jack Straw Writers Program started off like a scrappy new kid on the block, but almost twenty years later, it's still showcasing new and established Seattle-dwelling writers.

Richard Hugo House was founded by Linda Jaech, Andrea Lewis, and Frances McCue in 1997. Frances was the first director, and I was the first person she and Linda hired. "We want you to be writer-in-residence," they said. "Do whatever you want." I'd been teaching in the University of Washington Extension program and in the Writers in the Schools program for Seattle Arts & Lectures, and all over the place, so having a place to do creative programming as a teacher made me happy and grateful. Like Jack Straw, Hugo House began as a scrappy alternative to the earnest, dappled-salmon Northwest-landscapy stuff or bad-imitation Beat stuff or well-behaved university stuff, which made up different Seattle writing communities back then. I'm glad these programs came along, glad they're still here, and looking forward to seeing the totally new, different, weird literary-type things the next generation or two come up with.

DOUG NUFER

ON READINGS AND OULIPO

For five years, Anna Mockler, Gregory Hischak, and I performed as Staggered Thirds. Each of us would write a spoken-word piece and then score it for three voices, and the voices would often overlap, like music, a play, or a cacophony that made sense. There were so many cues that to look up from the page was to risk getting hopelessly lost.

We played bars and cafés, theaters and a hotel room, arts festivals and reading series. My favorite gigs were at the Little Theater on Nineteenth Avenue East, when it was run by the Northwest Film Forum.

On the day of one show in February 2001, I went to the theater to make some arrangements, and while I was talking to Kat, the office manager, everything started to wobble. We ran outside and watched the bus wires whipping the air. Bricks from the back of the theater filled the alley, but the building wasn't condemned.

Events were canceled all over town right after the Nisqually earthquake, so friends with tickets to other shows came to ours.

We rolled out the bar on stage. The concession prices were an intelligence test: two dollars for one cup of wine; five dollars for a bottomless cup of endless refills. Among the wines were samples of various Rhône and Bordeaux reds from distributors to my wine shop, and magnums of Brunello I had bought at closeout. At some point, with everyone milling around and drinking and yacking, it occurred to me that we had a show to do.

We also would perform at the Little Theater with a music act following us. The Wally Shoup trio—with Reuben Radding on bass, Bob Rees on drums, and Wally on sax—did wild improv jazz. Avant-whatever music consortiums and experimental poetry enterprises often scrounge for ways to draw outside of their specialized audiences, and we thought that it would be a good ploy for each of us to tap into the other group's followers. This worked especially well when we inadvertently gave two different starting times to the show, so we doubled the house, as the poetry crowd came early and the music crowd came late. I remember sitting in the office with the music blasting through the wall, giddily sifting through piles of money. Even after we paid the rent, each of the six of us would take home, like, fifty dollars. And I thought, hey, you know, this art thing can really pay off.

In 1987, the year that *Life A User's Manual* by Georges Perec, came out in English, Invisible Seattle brought Harry Mathews and Jacques Roubaud, Perec's fellow members of the French avant-garde literary society Oulipo, to the Elliott Bay Book Company. The ostensible reasons for why these two writers would travel to Seattle from Paris had to do with the Invisible Seattle Constitution Project and with the writers' recently published novels, but as far as I was concerned, Oulipo came to Seattle to save my life as a writer.

Invisible Seattle was a group of writers and artists who collaborated on projects throughout the '80s and beyond. For the Constitution Project, participants made up or came up with various constitutions after consulting (or simply stealing from) sources of regulations, rules, and mission statements. In order to gather material for *Invisible Seattle: The Novel of Seattle, by Seattle* (perhaps the first crowdsourced novel—before "crowdsourcing" was even a word), group members dressed as construction workers with question marks on their hard hats to collect data by conducting surveys at the 1983 Bumbershoot festival.

Before the 1987 visit, I learned all I could about Oulipo (which stands for Ouvroir de Littérature Potentielle, translated as Workshop of Potential Literature) and how members of this group invented and rediscovered formal constraints to make them write in ways they otherwise couldn't have imagined. Thanks to Philip Wohlstetter of Invisible Seattle, I got to meet the Oulipians, drive them around, and have dinner with them. Their crazy methods appealed to me. I had tried to write in other ways; why not give their way a try?

It seemed that writers from all over were always coming to Elliott Bay, and that however much a writer here might identify with writers from other parts of the world, we would often be subjected to proclamations of what Seattle writing was, is, and ought to be, as if one had to choose to be a Northwest writer. More than other places I have lived, Seattle seems to me to be an open city, a place open to "potential literature."

TERI HEIN

ON NORTHWEST BOOKFEST
AND THE HUTCH SCHOOL

It was 1995, and I had agreed to help my friend Kitty Harmon on her (brilliant) idea: the Northwest Bookfest. Why she thought curmudgeonly Teri Hein would make a good diva for the author hospitality room is beyond me, although I'm nothing if not reliable. My job, with a team of volunteers, was to make all visiting authors feel loved, hydrated, transported, fed, and oriented while they waited for their panel, signing, or appearance onstage in that lovely yet wildly drafty building at Pier 48. Most complicated was organizing airport transportation for the hundred-odd authors who came into town. I had a small army of volunteer drivers who had assiduously vacuumed dog hair and topped off tanks to collect authors flying in at all times of day or night from all parts of the country. When I could, I picked authors up myself, and I have stories of Anita Hill maneuvering her way into my red Jeep Wrangler in her pencil skirt, and Joyce Carol Oates marveling at the vehicle, which she apparently had never seen the likes of. Perhaps my most memorable day was when both Studs Terkel and Ken Kesey were arriving on the same afternoon. Ken's wife, who seemed to serve also as a quasi-manager, in the way spouses often do, requested that someone "very responsible" pick up Ken (that would be me). At the same time, I realized Studs's plane was arriving painfully close to his performance time, so I needed a fast but safe, punctual driver (that would be my partner, Jim). While I was picking up Ken (easy to spot in his rainbow coat, red pants, and red beret) and driving him north in my red Jeep, Jim was picking up Studs in a former police car—Jim had bought at an auction, complete with spotlight and back doors that wouldn't open from the inside. Jim located Studs at the airport, quickly got him back to his car, and then, to Jim's shock, realized he had a flat tire . . . and not much time. With the speed of lightning, Jim changed the tire while Studs, who had never even driven a car, watched with fascination. Tire changed, they both leapt in the car and sped north. Studs, ever the master interviewer, quizzed Jim all the way up I-5 on his life as a commercial fisherman and art collector. Upon arriving at the hospitality room, Jim (covered with grease) introduced me to Studs, who marveled at Jim's tire-changing aptitude. Then I introduced Studs to Ken (leading to some moments of mutual admiration), and Studs insisted that Ken and I meet Jim and him for dinner later.

So that is how Ken Kesey and I ended up at Ray's Boathouse at nine o'clock that night, where we found at a long table Studs Terkel, nonagenarian environmentalist Hazel Wolf, social justice activist Aki Kurose, and my Jim. Studs had just published his book *Coming of Age: The Story of Our Century by Those Who've Lived It* and was wining and dining two of the subjects in his book—all at least seventy years old, and both lovers of martinis and good conversation. Jim (in his late fifties) and Ken (just sixty) and me (in my early forties) were the pups at the end of the table. As I recall, each elder, to a one, was fairly deaf, so conversation was loud, with great collegiality. I remember it as a night of great laughter, great martinis, and a chorus of "What?" "What?" "What?" punctuated by the remarkably infectious laugh of Studs Terkel.

I remember seeing (through my martini haze) at one end of the table Studs Terkel, a man who with his interviews and writing had captured for decades the lives of common (and not-so-common) people in the most essential ways, and at the other end Ken Kesey, whose own life was considered far from common and whose own writing had brilliantly captured the essence of what it is to be a human alive in the world. Between them were sandwiched the very people who inspire writing: this group of elderly, dynamic, and very accomplished people who had lived their lives on their own terms and survived long enough to reflect back on it. Memorable, yes.

It was 2000, I think, and I was a teacher at the Hutch School, a school for patients in Seattle for several months for cancer treatment, and their family members. My memoir, *Atomic Farmgirl*, relates my own experiences with cancer in my neighborhood growing up in the Palouse of Eastern Washington. Dave Eggers had come to town to promote his memoir, *A Heartbreaking Work of Staggering Genius*, which details his parents' death from cancer and his subsequent life raising his younger brother. Dave had asked our mutual friend Rick Simonson from the Elliott Bay Book Company if there was a school where he could teach a writing workshop when he came to town. Hence, Dave came to the Hutch School, where he treated my high-school class at the time to a haiku poetry workshop. It was a lovely afternoon of writing, reading, and telling life stories. And Dave invited the whole class to come to his reading that evening at Elliott Bay as his special guests.

They were a motley crew, as I recall. Roy from Vancouver, an outpatient allowed to attend the Hutch workshop, carried a respirator on his shoulder, which clicked and wheezed through the whole session. Because he had no immune system to speak of, he wasn't allowed by his doctors to attend the reading that night. Renata, a member of the Hopi tribe from Arizona who rarely uttered a word, found out in the middle of the workshop that her older brother, the patient in her family, had relapsed posttransplant—a devastating blow. However distraught, she chose to go to Dave's reading anyway, and I agreed to pick her up in front of the hospital where her brother was an inpatient. There were Kate and Alison, sisters from North Carolina whose father, a forest ranger, was a patient. There were three siblings from Mississippi whose father was also a patient, a career military man. And North, a kid from Alaska, aptly named, who'd had three bone marrow transplants and, like Roy, couldn't risk the reading. There must have been about ten of us who went downtown. It was an odd outing for a bunch of kids who despite the tragedies of life were having their own kind of adventure living here in Seattle.

Not a one of my students had ever heard of Dave Eggers, but he was a fun workshop teacher and offered them something to do that wasn't about hanging around a hospital in the evening with their seriously ill family members.

As we pulled up to the bookstore, we noted a line around the block three to four people thick waiting to get in. Alison asked, "Is that line for *our* Dave?"

The bookstore was brimming with people in a fire-code-nervous-packed kind of way. And all for "our Dave," who had reserved the front row for the Hutch School kids, dedicated the evening to them, read some of the haikus they had written that day, and even read some of their work from a copy of their school newspaper, the *Hutch Times*, which he had randomly picked up from a table at the school. People were very receptive to their writing, and afterward, as the crowd was filtering out, many stopped the students to tell them how meaningful their writing was. My students felt like movie stars or heroes or definitely what they were: kids far from home being treated like somebodies in this packed basement bookstore in Seattle, Washington.

I feel safe saying that the evening is still embedded in the minds of my students. I would think what struck them is how powerful or entertaining or captivating their own words were when delivered by a competent reader to a receptive audience. And while Dave was obviously famous and "movie-starry" (as one of the students noted when we returned to the van), he was also just a regular guy, which I think somehow made their own futures as writers that much more imaginable.

MIA LIPMAN

Founder, Lit Fix Reading and Music Series

BRINGING THE BAY TO THE SOUND

When I moved to Seattle after almost a decade and a half in the Bay Area, I wanted to get involved in the literary community as soon as possible—I was deeply ingrained in that world in San Francisco, so leaving felt like severing a creative limb. I'd also been devoting a huge amount of editorial and emotional energy to *Canteen*, the literary magazine I founded with friends about eight years ago, so I felt burned out on desk work and ready to spend time with writers in person instead. We'd put on a bunch of readings and fund-raisers for *Canteen*, so curating a series in my new city seemed like a natural step. I figured it would help me get out of the house and find my people.

RAIN, FLEECE, AND GREEN SPACE

Leaving San Francisco was the hardest move I've ever made, but Lit Fix has eased the way. I knew Seattle would live up to its reputation for coffee, rain, fleece, and green space. What I didn't expect was how generous and openhearted its writers would be.

READINGS ALL OVER TOWN

After a year or so of going to readings all over town—especially at Hugo House and Town Hall—I started to recognize faces and feel brave enough to say hello. Then, at Lit Crawl Seattle in 2012, I had the great luck to be crawling through the rain with Jane Ganahl, cofounder of San Francisco's Litquake festival and the mother of all literary connectors. She began introducing me to just about everyone we saw, and I realized it was time to put my fanciful idea about a series into motion. At the Seattle7Writers event, Sean Beaudoin killed it with a hilarious piece about zombies, and I decided he was the first person I'd ask to read at my nascent series (especially appropriate because I wanted music in the mix, and Sean knows a thing or two about that art form as well).

So I found Sean's website and wrote to him blind. Not only did he agree to read at a series that didn't exist yet, run by a person he'd barely met, but he also recommended a dozen other authors. I reached out to some of them, they connected me to more people, and the wheel rolled from there. Peter Mountford gave my name to a fellow series organizer in Hawaii who was putting together a panel for AWP. Brian McGuigan told me about other series in town I should check out. Both of them have read at Lit Fix too.

Lit Fix is coming up on three years as a series, and nearly every author I've asked to take part has said yes. Same for every singersongwriter and band that's been asked to play. And all the performers donate their time and talent, so proceeds from the door can go to local organizations that support literacy.

RUGGED, SEXY STORIES OF SURVIVAL

A former coworker of mine, Jason Kirk, is a local editor and poet. He developed a passion for haiku—admittedly not my favorite kind of poetry—and pitched the idea of reading his new work at Lit Fix in December 2013. He'd never given a public haiku performance, and I wasn't sure how it would go over. Haiku loves spring, and it tends toward wistfulness and delicacy. In Seattle in winter, people want whiskey and meat on their bones. They want hats and sweaters and rugged, sexy stories of survival.

But Jason is a friend, and neither of us had anything to lose, so haiku it was. In front of the biggest audience Lit Fix had ever seen, Jason took the stage with no notes, pulled the mike off the stand, strutted his haiku all over the Rendezvous, and brought the house down. It was awesome. I can't say it made me into a haiku convert, but for those fifteen minutes, I believed.

SEATTLE WRITER WHO DESERVES MORE ATTENTION

Corinne Manning writes exceptionally wry, smart, funny short pieces, and she's very comfortable and engaging with audiences. I've seen her read a few times and always wished she would keep going. I'd be first in line to buy a story or essay collection by Corinne.

BEST LITERARY PERFORMER

Imani Sims gave a fantastic reading last year at Cheap Wine & Poetry, one of the regular series at Hugo House. She has incredible stage presence and performs poetry with her whole self, voice and body. By the end, we were all leaning forward in our seats to absorb the energy she was offering us.

BEST NEIGHBORHOOD TO SET A MURDER MYSTERY

I'd love to read a mystery set in Lake City, most likely because I'm usually listening to *This American Life* when I drive through it. It makes me wonder what kind of darkness is lurking behind the pet stores, auto dealerships, and strip joints.

BEST NEIGHBORHOOD TO SET A SCIENCE-FICTION NOVEL

The stretch of Alaskan Way beneath the Viaduct construction project feels like prime sci-fi territory. All those Pioneer Square ghosts and tech start-ups have to meet in the middle somewhere, and it's not hard to imagine otherworldly life forms touching down in the Olympic Sculpture Park or beaming up the Great Wheel.

NEIGHBORHOOD BOOKSTORE OF CHOICE

Elliott Bay, all the way. The last book I bought there was John Cleese's *So, Anyway . . .* , but this question reminds me that my nephew's birthday is coming up. Time to do a little shopping!

BEST DAY JOB FOR A WRITER IN SEATTLE

Most Seattle writers I know do something tangentially or directly related to writing as their day jobs: teaching, editing, freelancing, the usual suspects. (Finding a partner with a corporate job is also a popular option, if you can swing it.) But if someone has invented a wildly lucrative new career that leaves most of the day free for creative work, please don't keep it to yourself.

RICK SIMONSON

ON THE ELLIOTT BAY BOOK COMPANY
AND HARUKI MURAKAMI

It was the fall of 1984, thirty years ago as this is written, that author readings began to happen in a consistent manner at the Elliott Bay Book Company. This was at our original Pioneer Square home, the corner of First Avenue South and Main Street. Intermittent readings, often in jerry-rigged setups, had happened before that, with Paul Hansen, Sam Hamill, Belle Randall, Connie Martin, Barry Lopez, R. Buckminster Fuller, Joseph Campbell, Lewis Hyde, and a few others along the way.

One of the store's many remodeling projects gave us a space that wasn't in the middle of ordinary bookstore or café foot traffic. Authors talking wouldn't "impose" on things, nor would things, save the clatter of the espresso machine, generally impinge on someone reading to people who were there to listen.

We decided to try it all out as a series—at that point once a week or so—and we presented it that way. As would be expected, most of those willing were from here, or near—poet Carol Jane Bangs of Port Townsend, poet Gary Holthaus (who often passed through) from Alaska, poet Sharon Doubiago (then somewhat vaguely based at various West Coast points, so far as I could tell, though Judith Roche knew how to find her), and Seattle poets and writers Colleen McElroy, Charles Johnson, and Ivan Doig.

All of this would be fine and good, and help set the tone for what happened in years to come. There has always been a strong local/regional scene for writers and presses based here. That first reading series also featured something else which has been part and parcel of things—that is, writers from seriously far away. Ebba Haslund and Tove Nilsen came to Seattle and Elliott Bay from their home country of Norway, part of a Norwegian government-sponsored tour to promote a translated anthology, *An Everyday Story*, edited and translated by Seattle's Katherine Hanson. It was published by renowned feminist publisher Seal Press, then based in Seattle.

Seal, with Barbara Wilson (now Barbara Sjoholm), Rachel da Silva, Faith Conlon, Holly Morris, and numerous others, was probably the most nationally significant Seattle-based press during the late '70s through the '90s, with books that helped change public language and behavior. Numerous authors Seal published would read or speak at Elliott Bay, including Scandinavian writers like Gerd Brantenberg. Especially memorable was Egyptian writer/activist Nawal El Saadawi, who packed the house the likes of which we had never seen before.

It was at an annual book convention, held in mid-1989 in Washington, DC, with sensory overload and little sleep, that I happened upon a booth for the Japanese publisher Kodansha, whose

US offerings we generally did well with—mostly books of crafts, gardening, and perhaps some cooking, art, or older literature. They were good books but not commanding my attention when so much more was. A spritely man named Elmer Luke (so his badge said) waylaid me. Maybe it was my badge, identifying me as being from a bookstore in Seattle, that inspired him to put in my hand a bright-blue-and-green paperback advance copy of a novel that he said was by "the Japanese Tom Robbins."

Later in the year this novel, *A Wild Sheep Chase*, was published. Japanese Tom Robbins or not, this first book of Haruki Murakami's to be translated and published in the United States did fine enough with us. It found a good number of readers. It found me. In the next few years, there would be other Murakami books—the novels *Hard-Boiled Wonderland and the End of the World* and *Dance Dance Dance*, and a book of stories, *The Elephant Vanishes*. We did well with all of these books. Readership grew. Word of mouth was at work.

Murakami had rock-star stature in his home country of Japan, where his new books could sell in the millions. Some of that seemed to be based on the way his work conflated conformist life in Japan yet appealed to a resistant streak of rebellion and individuality. His work often had mystery at its core. It also piqued my curiosity to read of his interest in Western writing and music, his familiarity extending to translating numerous American writers into Japanese—Raymond Carver, Grace Paley, and Tim O'Brien among them.

Murakami's work had grown in popularity—and yet, I would learn, not *so* much more. This was driven home when I saw an editorial "tip sheet" produced by Knopf as it set about publishing the novel *The Wind-Up Bird Chronicle* in 1997. This sheet had information about the book that would appear later in the Knopf seasonal catalogue, or on the dust flap of the book cover. But what I remember were the sales numbers. None of his books had yet exceeded ten thousand copies sold in hardcover in the United States.

By the time Knopf published *The Wind-Up Bird Chronicle*, its first Murakami novel, a conversation about writers from abroad visiting Seattle had been set in motion. We had heard that Murakami would be in the United States, that his time was limited, but, yes, Seattle was possible. Among our allies in this wooing was poet Tess Gallagher, who knew Murakami and his wife, Yoko, because Murakami had translated the work of Tess's late husband, Raymond Carver. Finally, arrangements for Seattle came to pass. His Elliott Bay evening would be the Tuesday of Thanksgiving week—usually not the most auspicious time for authors. People are often distracted, in holiday mode. We've known our share of disappointingly small audiences at such times.

With Murakami, we knew we'd have an audience—based on his readership—but no inkling of how many there would be. He seemed to be a favorite writer of many who would say, "I have this favorite writer that almost no one else here knows about: Haruki Murakami." In those days before social media, before Internet connectivity, readers thought they were more "alone" this way. We knew those readers were there and that they constituted a good audience. They would find each other come the night, we thought.

A *Seattle Times* profile piece that ran before his Elliott Bay evening may have helped get the word out even more, certainly to some different quarters. Whatever. Word got out. Those who came to the bookstore that November night thinking that they and a hardy few others who knew about this amazing writer would constitute some intimate cluster of people had their eyes opened.

Elliott Bay's basement was packed—and then some. The reading room, the café adjoining. People in spaces and places where they wouldn't be able to see but could at least hear. Many clutched Japanese-language editions. Their presence—and reaction—were especially astounding. Here they were in a place utterly remote and distant from Japan, and here was this literary icon, in fairly close quarters, who didn't do this kind of thing in Japan, but here would hold forth, sign books, and greet people. How could this be?

Beforehand, serenely above it all, literally, in an upstairs office, Murakami and Yoko visited with Tess Gallagher. All relaxed and congenial, catching up on this and that. Some logistics were discussed—namely, who would say what and in what languages.

It was something to stand on that small stage in that basement room and feel this intense energy and attention. On a night like that, you feel the immensity and closeness of the world all at once. Readers from far away alongside readers from Seattle.

Murakami spoke for a bit in English, then read a portion of *Nejimaki-dori kuronikuru*, as *The Wind-Up Bird Chronicle* is originally known, in Japanese. I then read a sequence of it in English, a passage I remember being very moved by, to give readers a feel for what translator Jay Rubin (then at Harvard, but previously at the University of Washington) had done in making it so marvelous. When it was time for questions, no one had any idea, seeing hands raised, what language the questions would come in. Some people asked questions in Japanese, including some who didn't appear Japanese. Others, who might have been Japanese, going by appearance, asked questions in English.

The Wind-Up Bird Chronicle would be the book of Murakami's that finally took off in the United States. Sales for Elliott Bay clearly went through the roof, but reviews and word of mouth picked up a momentum that has not abated with the books and years since.

Having hosted Haruki Murakami in that packed, overflowing basement space when he was still selling fewer than ten thousand copies of his novels in hardcover, I can only imagine what a crowd he would attract now. No space in Seattle short of one of the big sports arenas or stadiums would be adequate. Readers now flock to Elliott Bay at midnight to buy copies of Murakami's books—like *1Q84* and *Colorless Tsukuru Tazaki and His Years of Pilgrimage*—the moment they are officially released. When I see readers wander in at midnight on a Monday when they should otherwise be in bed, all in anticipation of a book and an author such as this, I remember that November night years ago, and the moment I was introduced to the work of the Japanese Tom Robbins. All for the long haul.

RACHEL KESSLER, SIERRA NELSON, AND SARAH PAUL OCAMPO

ON THE TYPING EXPLOSION

Sarah Paul Ocampo:

Some might call The Typing Explosion a literary-performance group or performance art, but it was more like a girl band with writers instead of musicians. It started as a one-off in 1998—I had just met Sierra, and I had known Rachel for a long time—so I invited them over to my apartment, and we all brought our typewriters. It was a really easy birth . . . I had the basic idea, and we sat down and worked out the rest. We performed the next week at Zeitgeist Coffee in Pioneer Square (at that time located in the Washington Shoe Building), thinking it would be a one-time performance. We ended up performing for over ten years.

Sierra Nelson:

There are so many moments that stand out from our years as the Dianes of The Typing Explosion. (When we went into our hive-mind typing pool to collaborate, each of us was named Diane. Not that anyone else knew that necessarily, as we didn't speak aloud during our typing sessions, and no one was allowed to speak to us, and we communicated only through poetry and our intricate system of bells, horns, and whistles. But having a secret identity helped us enter that collaborative-performance space.)

Sarah Paul Ocampo:

The Typing Explosion consisted of writing poetry on demand, usually writing three poems at a time. There were rules displayed on an overhead projector that had to be followed, in order for audience members to receive their poems, and a massive black shredder that would be used if you didn't follow the rules.

Sierra Nelson:

We had borrowed a giant Shredmaster—a truly horrifying-looking machine, heavy, looked like it might eat a finger—and if anyone broke our posted rules (many of which were borrowed from the pool: no shoving, no spitting, etc.) their poem-in-progress would be shredded. Mischievous friends would sometimes threaten to break a rule or mess with us, but people rarely did. Once they got there, people *wanted their poem*—when you see it being created right before your eyes, just for you, you want to know what it says. The fact that people rarely broke the rules I think speaks to the underlying thrill of poetry—what we hoped people would discover or remember from our shenanigans. We lured them in with the hoopla of our vintage costumes (this was before *Mad Men*), the clamor of our communiqués, and the electric pounding thrum of typewriters—but what was cranked out of our colorful machine was intimate, subversive, tactile, and person-to-person.

Sarah Paul Ocampo:

Participants had the choice of selecting a poem title we had typed and filed in a card catalogue, or they could write their own title. No title would ever be repeated. Each of us contributed to the poem—there was no pattern or routine for who wrote what. We spoke to each other through sounds and had a paper-passing technique that mimicked a secretarial corps de ballet. Each poem was dated and notarized by us, and signed for by the recipient. We kept the carbon copy and they got the original.

Sierra Nelson:

All of our mothers had been typists at one point in their careers; it was a job that many women found was the only work they could get in the '50s and '60s, and the anonymous typing pool of seemingly interchangeable women could be especially grim. We wanted to shed light on that history and also to upend it. We weren't typing what you wanted: we were typing what we and the poem wanted. What you got was what you got; it was punk like that.

Sarah Paul Ocampo:

Sierra was the first secretary that the audience member would be introduced to in the lineup. She was the blonde—the happy-go-lucky, best-foot-forward, right-away-sir secretary. She took the title and started the poem.

Rachel, the redhead, sat in the middle. She was known as the zany one, the firecracker, the wild card. She had a whistle and kept us on track with our "union breaks," clocking us in and out.

I was the brunette—the dark cloud, the office vamp at the end of the line. I stamped the completed poem with The Typing Explosion Union Local 898 stamp, dated it, and had the audience member sign it. Oftentimes we would pin the carbons behind us on outstretched pantyhose. (It was pretty grotesque, really.)

The Dianes all played different parts in pushing the poem through. Over the ten-plus years we performed, we calculated we typed about five thousand original poems.

After a few years of the sit-down typing, we ended up getting some grants and then branching out into theater installations and recordings. It was theater, it was sound, and it was writing. We performed with musicians, artists, dancers, drag queens . . . in bars, libraries, movie theaters, bookstores, art galleries.

Rachel Kessler:

I remember performing in Venice during the Biennale. It was the summer that hundreds, if not thousands, of old people dropped dead all across Europe from temperatures of 104 and on up. Nowhere was there air-conditioning. We were strolling around in a semihallucinatory state with our typewriters strapped to our chests (thanks to the beautiful cigarette-girl boxes John DeShazo made us), typing poems for people. An elegant older Italian woman came up to us and complimented our fashion, praising us especially for wearing pantyhose, regardless of the heat. I felt very proud, having impressed this beautiful woman, as the world dipped and swayed in fever.

Sarah Paul Ocampo:

San Francisco, the early aughts. We were performing at the Beauty Bar in the Mission. It was a great place for us, as the vibe was throwback and you could get your nails done while having a martini. Rachel and I stepped out to have a smoke when a bike messenger rode by and spit on Rachel and yelled, "Fucking yuppie!" Rachel, who I recall was wearing a pink wool two-piece skirt suit, her hair in an updo, yelled back, "I'm a secretary! From the sixties!" The injustice.

Sierra Nelson:

A collage of highlights from the years:

Typing outside for the tens of thousands who attended Bumbershoot. Some people waited in line for *hours* for a poem, and at one point it started to rain and Rachel's electric typewriter started sending out sparks.

The Wave Books Poetry Bus tour. It was a literal bus that rolled into town with "Poetry Bus" written on its side, picking up and dropping off poets throughout North America, fifty cities in fifty days. The Typing Explosion did the Toronto to upstate New York leg, ending at DIA:Beacon. I remember a bemused John Ashbery getting up to the podium after we performed one night in DIA:Chelsea and saying, "Those ladies are a tough act to follow."

Typing followed by waltzing in the ballroom of the historic *Kalakala* ferry, rain falling into buckets all around us, coming in through the holes in the boat's ceiling and sides. That futuristic nautical behemoth operated from 1935 to 1967 and, in its prime, was featured at the 1962 Seattle World's Fair.

Performing at a Wieden+Kennedy party where Erykah Badu was the headliner, and a business guy creepily leering as he said, "Will you be my little secretary?"—as if nothing had actually changed in gender and power dynamics since the '50s.

The surprise of sold-out shows at the On the Boards studio for *Dear Diane*—our first full-length theater piece, the script of which was based entirely on our collaborative poems written over the years. Directed by Jamie Hook and with stunning set design by Kathryn Rathke, it showed a day in the life of the typing Dianes: from waking up together in their shared bed with a rock band sleeping underneath, to sharing a brown-bag lunch with the audience, and later overthrowing Bossy-Boss, played by the incredible Sarah Harlett, to write poetry in solidarity in a kind of surrealist-socialist revolt. One key ingredient in that *Dear Diane* show was a magical polar-bear character that would bring the Dianes cocktails when they went to the swimming pool of their minds (with a tiny replica of a motel pool pulled from the filing cabinet) or offer hugs in the ladies' lounge. In fact, this same polar-bear costume has played a part in many facets of Seattle's cultural history and is on display at MOHAI.

In our commissioned cabaret show, *Love, Exciting Love*, at Capitol Hill Arts Center (in the building that now houses Velocity Dance Center), we explored "154 kinds of love," most of them expressed through original songs and each with a different costume. In one part of the show, my then-eighty-year-old grandmother, Grandma Green—who had led quite a life and was known among friends for her psychic abilities—took live calls from our audience to answer love-life questions. I remember one gentleman—a local TV celebrity, in fact—asking if he would ever find love. Grandma Green started with some solid practical advice ("Do the things that *you* enjoy," "Sometimes love is slow and there isn't any reason"), but she ended with the pronouncement that if he was patient she could see love coming his way. A year later, we read in the paper that he was engaged!

Sarah Paul Ocampo:
I was working at Zeitgeist when the phone rang. I picked up, and the guy said he was calling from *USA Today*'s arts section, and he asked for me, Sarah Paul Ocampo. I thought it had to be some kind of joke; I didn't even know that *USA Today* had an arts section. They'd read about us in a *Seattle Times* article that had been picked up by the Associated Press. They sent out a very thoughtful interviewer and did a color photo with a two-page article. We were crossing our arms in the picture with our "Rules" projected across our faces. We couldn't have imagined this attention. At the

time, we were actually losing money each time we typed (because of cabs, paper, ribbons, nylons). We didn't have a manager, so we were trying not to pee our pants when we started getting interviews with *Spin*, *Jane*, *Mademoiselle*, *Bust*, *Sunset*, and *Allure*.

The day before a guy from *People* magazine came to interview us, we had done this amazing '60s girl band–inspired photo shoot (a whole lotta beehives) with a great photographer they'd sent out. The next day the interviewer showed up to meet us two hours late, which I remember was a real drag because we had taken off work/gotten a babysitter to make this happen. The guy asked us why we didn't have management and basically told us we'd never make it big if we stayed in Seattle. At this point, we told him he was an asshole, paid our tab with our tip money, and left. They never ran that article (or those photos!).

Rachel Kessler:

I remember an amazing burlesque show/reading with Michelle Tea that we performed in at the Speakeasy in Belltown. We opened with the opposite of burlesque, where I played a manual loop on an Unwound record while we all slowly put on our pantyhose. Like maybe nothing was happening and it took a very long time. The room was so quiet. Then we typed a lot of dirty poems, as per our participant's requests. They were quiet but inside their minds they were filthy. Which reminds me of a terrifying performance in Bellevue where we stared at the audience as if they were our mirror while applying lipstick and the drunk husband of a journalist who we had offended started heckling us, like an irate mom idling in the station wagon: "WHAT are you DOING?

WHAT is taking you so long?" Without blinking, Sarah Paul stared and honked her horn at him, somewhere out there in the darkened theater.

But good things can happen in Bellevue too. Our first audio poetry installation piece "Salon" premiered at the Bellevue Art Museum. We turned three hairdryer chairs into interactive sound sculptures, surrounded by the rest of the detritus of a hair salon from the late 1960s: handbags stuffed with what looked like rain bonnets and coupons that were actually poems, magazines that we had hacked and made into poems, as well as one hundred different nail polish jars labeled with our own invented color names, such as "Minimum Wage Red," that made a list poem.

Sierra Nelson:

One of my favorite performances as The Typing Explosion was outside Bailey/Coy Books on Valentine's Day 2003, I believe. It was freezing cold; I don't think there was snow, but it felt on the verge, a rare thing for Seattle. We were bundled in late '50s wool suits outside the store's big front windows on Broadway, and probably wearing some of the elegant coats Rachel had inherited from her grandmother. I remember it was a weekday and we were typing in the early evening, so people could get love poems on their way home from work: our valentine to Seattle. We debuted our hand-made *Thirteen Love Poems and One Ugly One* book that night to sell in the store, but the part I remember most was cranking out those new originals on our Smith Coronas for all the lovers and loners until it got too dark to see.

Sarah Paul Ocampo:

More than being a "literary-performance group," I felt like we were in a band. A band of sister writers. We weren't thinking about what we were doing; we were just doing it. Nobody told us we couldn't, or if they did, we didn't listen. We just kept saying yes. We went from doing nonverbal "type-ins" to creating evening-length theater pieces and installations, to publishing several chapbooks and touring the country, as well as performing with bands, artists, poets, dancers, and anyone else who seemed like a good time.

Rachel Kessler:

During the years we collaborated as The Typing Explosion, I got pregnant and had two small kids. Finding '60s secretarial maternity garb was hilarious. It seemed like I was always either pregnant or sporting a broken arm or ankle, or both. We showed up for an interview with *USA Today* with a baby in a buggy—I was broke and couldn't afford a babysitter. Making art with toddlers and infants suckling is challenging, and I do not know if I would have continued if it hadn't been for this collaboration. Sierra and Sarah Paul would come over to my snot-encrusted apartment and joggle babies while we worked. We'd stick the baby in the ExerSaucer, and Ruby, at that time a toddler, would watch us rehearse, offering sage directorial advice: "Too much talking." When we were overwhelmed with babies, we just stuck them in the show. Iris, as a four-month-old, appeared in *Merry Christmas, Anyway* as a sort of baby Jesus. When she started crying onstage, I nursed her briefly under my costume, then, after the scene, handed her off to my friend Mishy, backstage, who also happened to be lactating.

My kids referred to my fellow Dianes, individually or as a team, as "Ser-Ser." We were this cult of three female typists, writing collaborative poetry, flanked by infant daughters.

Sarah Paul Ocampo:

Occasionally, we had the opportunity to perform somewhere where the stakes felt a little higher. One of those times was performing for girls at King County Juvenile Detention. We had little time to load in and out, so we came dressed in our '60s secretarial outfits. We went through the metal detector, got patted down—a guard counted our props and extras before we sat down to type. At first . . . nothing. But then one girl jumped in and seemed to break the spell. Later the librarian told us that girl was kind of in charge of the group, and if she hadn't given her approval, we would've been sitting there without anyone participating for the duration. Like most titles that people wrote for themselves, the titles they wrote were personal: "The Chola That the Homies Call La Tiny," "Baby Daddy," "Cutter." Afterward, we did a quick Q&A, and a woman asked us if we were hiring—we took that as a big compliment. As a side note, while the female inmates were being led out after the show so the males could come into the library, a good-looking (I'm guessing) seventeen-year-old lifted up his shirt, showed me his twenty-four-pack, and whispered to me, "I want you to remember this." Okay . . . I will . . . Um, I do. Thank you.

Rachel Kessler:

We went on this epic tour of the King County Library System (who knew our county stretches all the way to Skykomish, Enumclaw,

Muckleshoot, and Algona-Pacific!) with death metal band BlöödHag, who have been known to throw copies of Octavia Butler and Philip K. Dick sci-fi novels at kids while playing. Somehow, by the powers of my Tetris mind, we packed all our typewriters, overhead projectors, screens, card catalog, and the Shredmaster among the baby car seats in an old hatchback clown car nearly every day of April (National Poetry Month). That was the most money we ever made. It was fantastic to roll into a small town, sample the deep-fried delights of their fast food drive-ins, and be the bizarre women making noise in the library. One day I decided to get an IUD installed during my lunch break (I had just given birth to my second kid, it seemed like a good cutoff point) and then went on to our scheduled library appearance that afternoon experiencing pretty intense cramping. Sierra and Sarah Paul made me a button that said, "Kiss me! I got my IUD today!"

BRIAN McGUIGAN

Cofounder, Cheap Wine & Poetry
and Cheap Beer & Prose

HOW IT ALL GOT STARTED

Steve Barker and I started the Cheap Wine & Poetry reading series in 2005, soon after we moved to Seattle. We were having trouble breaking into the literary community. We were in our early twenties, and nobody was taking us seriously. At the time, the literary community was pretty fractured, particularly the poets. Everyone ran in their own circles. Neither Steve nor I were very cliquish, so we decided to start something of our own. If we couldn't work our way into the existing community, we thought, we'd just create a new one.

Back then, we were fresh out of college and broke, so we drank a lot of cheap wine and wrote lots of poetry. The combination made sense. We also wanted to create a series that didn't just draw poets and writers, but people who liked to have a good time. Hence, the glasses of wine for a buck. If people don't like poetry, we figured they'd at least like getting drunk for a handful of dollars. The first reading we did was in May 2005, and it was so packed we ran out of chairs. That night, we knew we'd invented something special.

PASS ME A BEER, BRO

A few years later, while we were drinking PBR in my backyard, Steve suggested we do the same thing but with beer. There weren't any reading series dedicated to showcasing prose writers only, so we decided to give it a shot. The first Cheap Beer & Prose, like the first CW&P, was packed. We killed the keg before the reading even began and had to run out and buy more. I always knew writers liked to drink, but that was beyond belief.

A "DORM-LIKE" ATMOSPHERE

The thing about both Cheap Wine & Poetry and Cheap Beer & Prose is that almost every reader gets huge applause—and many get big laughs. The crowd is always warm and supportive, and the old dorm-like atmosphere of the Hugo House cabaret is conducive to having a good time. I'm sure the cheap stuff has something to do with it too. The biggest applause I can remember was a night when David Schmader (of the *Stranger*) presented a multimedia essay about the tragic death of his dog, a Boston terrier mix named Diane. The piece was both hilarious and heart-wrenching, and it ended with Dave bringing Diane's sister onstage, an adorable dog named Bunny, who lip-synched Fleetwood Mac to close the night out. It was one of those nights where everyone in the crowd laughed until they cried.

"DON'T SUCK"

At the very first Cheap Beer & Prose, Maria Semple read from *Where'd You Go, Bernadette*. This was back before the book had been published. Before the reading, she'd confessed to me that she was nervous to read from it. I assured her she'd be great, but the truth was, I told every writer that. What kind of curator would I be if I said, "Well, don't suck"? Maria nervously took the stage with a huge three-ring binder under her arm. She read from several sections lampooning

Seattle, Microsofties, and the city's famed five-way intersections. By the end, we all knew the book she hadn't yet finished was going to be a hit.

CRYING AND/OR PEEING ON YOURSELF

The first time Johnny Evison read at Cheap Beer & Prose was shortly after his first novel, *All About Lulu*, had come out. He was trying to sell another book and invited the reps from Algonquin to the reading to see him in action. I don't know if it was nerves or what, but Johnny was putting back PBR tallboys. By the time he took the stage, he was noticeably drunk. Before he began reading, he confessed that ever since he'd had kids he'd become a bit of a crier, and he'd had enough to drink already that he'd either cry or piss himself, possibly onstage if all went as planned. Of course, the crowd loved it, and once he launched into his reading from what would be his third novel, *The Revised Fundamentals of Caregiving*, he had them eating out of his hand.

UM, THANKS . . . GRANDPA?

The most absurd and hilarious thing to ever happen at Cheap Wine or Cheap Beer was a reading by storyteller Jennifer Jasper. She took the stage with two bags and asked the audience to choose one, though she wouldn't tell us the contents of either. The audience chose the bigger bag, and Jennifer proceeded to tell a story about coming out to her grandfather, something she'd been worried about for fear of judgment. Her grandfather was a man's man, a woodworker, not the kind of guy you'd expect to be accepting of his granddaughter's homosexuality. But to Jennifer's surprise, he was totally supportive, and to show his love, he carved her something. Jennifer then whipped a giant knobby wooden dildo out of the bag, and the audience lost its shit. I don't think I've ever heard a room of people laugh so hard in my life.

THE ONE BOOK BY A SEATTLEITE TO PUT IN THE HANDS OF A VISITOR

Where'd You Go, Bernadette by Maria Semple. I'm not sure if it's the city's wealth of intelligence or its Scandinavian roots, but Seattle sometimes takes itself too seriously. *WYGB*, Semple's second novel, puts Seattle on its head, turning everything about the city—from its antisocial techies to its poorly gridded streets—into hilarious satire. No book by a local author has made me laugh out loud so much. Beyond the yuks, the novel is extremely well plotted, which makes it a perfect read for one of the many rainy days we have here.

SEATTLE WRITER WHO DESERVES MORE ATTENTION

Elissa Washuta. Elissa is a young, extremely talented writer. Her memoir, *My Body Is a Book of Rules*, should be required reading for anyone in their twenties. She tackles issues like mental illness, binge-drinking, and acquaintance rape with a mixture of honesty and insight that's well beyond her years. The memoir is also incredibly inventive. She pushes the boundaries of form in memoir to new places, reimagining *Law & Order* scripts and hilariously footnoting her own Match.com profile. She's definitely a writer to watch.

BEST LITERARY PERFORMER

Sherman Alexie, by far. I've seen him read several times. The most memorable reading I've seen him give was as part of the Hugo Literary Series. We asked him to write something new on the theme "While You Were Sleeping." He wrote a stunning piece about nightmares, his father, and growing up on the rez. Truly, we laughed and we cried. Sherman never fails to impress, but that night he was the Michael Jordan of literature, a reference I know he'll appreciate as a hoops fan.

BEST NEIGHBORHOOD TO SET A SCIENCE-FICTION NOVEL

Fremont would be the best for a sci-fi novel. The Troll, the Lenin statue, the naked people on bicycles—is there any better fodder?

BEST NEIGHBORHOOD TO SET A MURDER MYSTERY

Pioneer Square. The old cobblestone streets, dark alleys, and brick buildings give the neighborhood a noirish feel.

NEIGHBORHOOD BOOKSTORE OF CHOICE

I might live in the only neighborhood of Seattle that doesn't have a bookstore, but one is opening soon a few blocks from me. I usually shop at Elliott Bay. The last book I bought there was Leslie Jamison's *The Empathy Exams.* When I read books, I make notes on index cards and stick them between the pages. *The Empathy Exams* is full of cards.

BEST DAY JOB FOR A WRITER IN SEATTLE

The best day job for a writer is writing. I don't mean technical writing or copywriting but actual writing. Cut back on your expenses. Apply like crazy for grants. Do whatever you can to make do with what you have so you can write. And if you can't afford that, do something as mindless as possible and save whatever you have left for the page.

PART 5

REFLECTING

MATTHEW SIMMONS

ON SHELVES

I participate in the underground economy of bookshelves. My small shelves fill up, and I resolve to get rid of them and trade up to larger ones. I find a friend giving away a large shelf for an even larger one—as their large shelves are filled—and I take that shelf and fill it with my books. I give away my small shelf to someone whose even smaller shelf has filled and needs to be traded away. The bookshelves of Seattle move from home to home to home.

I drove to Seattle in a white Ford automobile loaded with my clothes and my CDs, but only a small number of books. I'd been picking them up and shedding them from move to move, from little Midwestern college town to little Midwestern college town. In Seattle, though, I found myself in the book trade—selling them, promoting them, writing them, letting their authors sleep on my couch—and that's when I began to acquire books in piles and stacks. Now, any move from one place in Seattle to another is a task that requires many, many medium-sized boxes—big enough for a good number of books, but not so many that the box is too heavy to carry. Everyone in town knows that formula—the one that yields the perfect book-moving box.

I can't imagine ever leaving here, if only because I wouldn't be able to move all my books. Seattle, city of literature, is a trap—a wonderful, lovely trap—where one cannot help but get burdened—happily, joyously burdened—with books from its many real, physical bookstores with its many real, physical book enthusiasts. Where every friend or stranger is a bookseller, everywhere you go someone has a suggestion of what to read next, and everyone's shelf either has space to spare or is about to be traded up for a newer shelf that does.

LARRY REID

Curator, Fantagraphics Bookstore & Gallery

BEST SECTION OF THE STORE

I'm particularly proud of our growing selection of self-published and small-press comix and zines. Our classic comic-strips section is another highlight. That said, we have a wonderfully diverse, yet cohesive collection of comix, graphics novels, and badass books.

ROCK STARS AND FORMER MAYORS

We see a lot of celebrities—particularly musicians—in our store. I'm inclined to protect their privacy. I can say that former mayor Mike McGinn was, and remains, a frequent visitor. He's a fan of graphic novels and he's passing that enthusiasm along to his children. He recently bought a copy of Art Spiegelman's *Maus* for his daughter.

A STORE THAT'S ALSO AN ARCHIVE

On rare occasion, I've realized a customer somehow located a rare out-of-print book that should remain in our archive. I've tried to gently persuade the patron to allow the book to stay, but I always defer to the customer's wishes.

DECEASED ARTISTS WHO ARE WELCOME TO GET
RESURRECTED AND VISIT THE FANTAGRAPHICS STORE

I'd love to spend some time with Winsor McCay, creator of the enchanting *Little Nemo in Slumberland* strip. Beyond that, I developed a close relationship with William S. Burroughs after I hosted a residency with him here in 1988 but lost contact in the years before he died. It'd be nice to somehow put closure to that. I would also like to meet up with former acquaintances Kurt Cobain and Jesse Bernstein and ask them to explain themselves.

THE ONE BOOK BY A SEATTLEITE TO PUT
IN THE HANDS OF A VISITOR

Buddy Does Seattle, Peter Bagge's cartoon chronicle of Seattle's grunge phenomenon is essential. This work, which collects the first fifteen issues of his *Hate* comic-book serial, helped define the attitudes and aesthetics of an international youth movement. A review by Bruce Barcott in 1994 suggests, "Twenty years from now, when people want to know what it was like to be young in 1990s Seattle, the only record we'll have is Peter Bagge's *Hate*." Twenty years later, that observation holds true.

SEATTLE GRAPHIC NOVELIST WHO DESERVES MORE ATTENTION

I'm fond of the work of Kelly Froh, who has been identified for too long as an "emerging artist." Her work is clever, sophisticated, and fully developed. There are also several young cartoonists who are primed to break out in the near future: Tom Van Deusen, Robyn Jordan, Max Clotfelter, Marc Palm, and Tatiana Gill, among others.

BEST LITERARY PERFORMER

Seattle cartoonist Ellen Forney is funny, charming, and wildly entertaining with her multimedia presentations.

MOST RIDICULOUS QUESTION A CUSTOMER EVER ASKED

After spending quite some time browsing the shelves, a visitor asked, "What is this place?"

BEST DAY JOB FOR AN ARTIST IN SEATTLE

I'm of the opinion that the best day job for any artist is being a self-employed artist. I fully recognize the sacrifice this involves. But I've seen too many young artists unwilling to make that leap of faith and finding themselves regretting it in later years.

SONORA JHA

ON SPINE & CROWN

I had never walked into this bookstore called Spine & Crown at 315 East Pine Street, a stone's throw away from my office at Seattle University. And yet, for more days and months and years than I know of, my heart hung out and grew several sizes among the aisles there.

I first learned of this when I called my son, Sahir, on his cell phone one day when he was late coming home from school. He would be leaving for college in a year or so, and I liked having him home for dinner.

He told me he was at Spine & Crown, browsing books. Okay, I said, and decided that dinner could be at eight instead of at six. In any case, it was mostly pizza in those days, because I was busy writing a book.

Another day, I called and he said he was at the bookstore again, speaking to someone called Chris.

"Who's Chris?" I asked.

"He owns and runs this bookstore," Sahir said.

Okay, I said. I could use the extra few hours to finish up the edits on my novel. The publisher had given me a tough deadline. And at least my son was out there reading books and talking about them.

For several months, this went on. Sahir would come home with little nuggets from conversations with Chris, the way other kids were going home with trophies from their after-school sporting events. He'd come home with books, like he always had, because that's what Seattle and I had raised him to do, but now all these books were purchased at Spine & Crown, recommended by their owner, not with a hard sell, but in meandering conversation.

"How old is this Chris?" I asked, taking care to sound nonchalant.

"Oh, he's much older than me," Sahir said. "He's a dad and all."

I imagined this "much older" Chris listening to my son blather on about books and the socialist politics that were now such a big part of his life. I thought of how that bookstore guy must, like me, be tuning my son out enough every now and then in order to get his work done. While he talked to my boy, I got the time to make phone calls and send e-mails to writers, requesting blurbs to promote my novel.

And, just because it is the thing that mothers must do, I Googled this guy who owned this bookstore. "Chris," I found out, was Kris Minta.

Oh. I had never actually asked Sahir how the man spelled his name. Kris was something of a literary legend in Seattle, Google told me. But, then, Sahir had already told me that Kris acquired books with a keen eye, the way no big bookstore could. Sahir had said, "We need people like Kris, who curate literary work for their city and feed the city in that way."

I decided I'd drop by sometime and check out Kris's bookstore. Weird that I frequented so many literary haunts in this city and I hadn't once thought to go to that store. Should I go when Sahir was there so he could introduce me to Kris? Or should I go when Sahir was at school so I could just go say "Hello, I'm Sahir's mom," and see if that name rang a bell for Kris or whether the bookstore wasn't where my boy had been hanging out after all? Immediately, I was ashamed. I had always trusted my son, and I wasn't going to start embarrassing him—or myself—with my mistrust now.

Then, one day, Sahir came home and told me that Spine & Crown was closing down, that the building was to be replaced with condos. "Once again in our world, efficiency will replace beauty," he said.

He told me also that Kris was going to leave the city. "But he's going to do something he's wanted to do for a while," Sahir said. "He's going to Syracuse to get an MFA and teach. I can see him really loving that," he said, smiling to himself.

"It's a good thing you're going off to college too," I said. "So you won't miss him." I had raised my son mostly as a single mom, and I had a habit of swooping in with "the sunny side" when he displayed the slightest hint of wistfulness.

"Oh, I'll miss him all right," Sahir said. "Kris has had a profound impact on my worldview. He's been one of the biggest influences in my life so far."

I knew, then, that I would never step into that bookstore or meet that man, not because I couldn't bear to share "influence" on my child's life with a stranger, but because this thing—this space and those books and those words—built a piece of this city that was my son's alone to have.

At the end of July that year, the bookstore closed and Kris moved to Syracuse. At the end of August, Sahir was gone to Swarthmore.

Today, as I write this piece, I call to tell my son about it. He's in Mumbai, where he is spending the summer volunteering, tutoring boys at a shelter, in English and math. "Please mention Magus Books in your essay, Mama," he says to me over the phone. "We must support that bookstore now. Can't let Magus close down, right?"

ZAPP
Zine Archive and Publishing Project

THE WORLD'S LARGEST ARCHIVE OF ZINES

The Zine Archive and Publishing Project (ZAPP) is a primarily volunteer-run community archive that consists of over thirty thousand zines. Over the past eighteen years, most, if not all, of these zines have been acquired through large and small donations, whether from vendors at the Portland Zine Symposium, from people looking to get rid of a box of zines that's been lying around in the garage, or from collectors/activists looking for a new, safe, and final home for their DIY treasures.

ZAPP is not just an archive of zines that the community can browse, though that's an integral facet of the zine library experience. It is also a place for people to discover that they can create zines too. ZAPP provides workshops and a workspace with materials to get the process started.

PRETZELS AND SHELLACKED BOLOGNA

ZAPP began as a little collection of about two hundred zines donated by Gary Greaves. From the get-go, ZAPP was a hotbed of activity and experimentation. One of our most prized zines, *Foreign Substance*, featured in our rare section, is one of a kind, handmade by Gary as part of a program he hosted for disadvantaged youth. The purpose of this weekly workshop was to boost self-esteem and encourage kids to exercise their creativity. *Foreign Substance* is an 8½ × 11 stapled zine of multicolored paper. The cover is dressed with pretzels, which spell part of the title, and a shellacked piece of bologna.

DIY ACADEMY

DIY Academy ran for only two years—in the summers of 2005 and 2006—but it is a bright, warm spot in the hearts of many who were involved. It was a product of ZAPP at a deeply important turning point in its history, when it became more than a collection of zines and expanded upon the do-it-yourself philosophy. DIY Academy was a series of five-dollar workshops, which included zine-making, to be sure, but also bike maintenance, vegan baking, self-defense, collage, and radio production. They ran for a whole month, and had virtually no budget and a handful of volunteers.

ZINES + A FIDDLE + A SAW

ZAPP has been known to step outside of the library, figuratively and literally, and into other avenues through performance. In the mid-2000s, ZAPP kicked off a tour at Hugo House, and went down the West Coast and back up again with a performing combination of zine-makers and a fiddle-and-saw duet. ZAPP just broke even after the tour was done, but it was worth the experience. In recent years, ZAPP has hosted multiple readings of touring zine-makers, including John Porcellino; Alex Wrekk, who hosts the Portland Zine Symposium every year; and local writers and artists.

ABSURD INSTRUCTIONS

In addition to performances and workshops, ZAPP, especially recently, has curated a number of exhibitions of the archive. One exhibition to note, in particular, was *Your Zine Is Alive and Well and Living in ZAPP*, shown in December of 2011. This exhibit's purpose was to play with the stringent regulations of observation in museums; volunteers built every display from found objects and fabricated a set of absurd instructions about how to interact with each one. It featured zines that spanned the twentieth century, including one of the oldest in the collection, from 1948. Many recently produced zines were displayed as well.

BEST NEIGHBORHOOD TO SET A MURDER MYSTERY

Ravenna during a summer LARPing (live action role-playing) tournament would be confusing and terrifying, because everyone is in costume and thus a great foundation for a successful murder mystery.

BEST NEIGHBORHOOD TO SET A SCIENCE-FICTION NOVEL

Cal Anderson Park on Capitol Hill could easily be the scene of a 4 a.m. alien abduction, in the basketball court or by the fountain. Volunteer Park, also on Capitol Hill, has a few different places that could easily facilitate a science-fiction plot, like the Conservatory, where a rat-eating Venus flytrap actually lives in real life, and let's not forget Edgar Allen Pew, the corpse flower.

CHARLES MUDEDE

ON JONATHAN RABAN

Over the past fifteen years or so, my habit has been to visit Jonathan Raban during fall or winter. I almost never see him in spring or summer. And so in my mind, his massive home (three floors), which is on the north side of Queen Anne Hill, is always in the dusk, always in the cold, always has a little yard that's covered by dead leaves, and a white, worn, and creaking gate that's been knocked out of ordinary time (our/animal/earth time) into the otherworld's time by the deep and wintry shadow of an old evergreen. An outdoor staircase ends at the home's main door on the second floor. Once inside, a wood-warm set of steps leads up to the third and final floor. This is where Raban entertains guests. There is something about this room that feels like the cabin of a ship. But I can never tell if this impression has to do with reality, with the actual facts of the furniture and design, or owes everything to Raban's books, all of which I have read, and many of which (including my favorite, *Passage to Juneau*) are about or involve sailing. This is also the floor with a bridge's view of Fremont and Ballard.

One evening in the winter of 2012 (ice on the little dark road leading to the gate, snow on the lawn between gate and stairs), Raban, who was born in Norfolk, England, in 1942, and who that night prepared a hearty lamb stew (spiced Indian style) and basmati rice, pointed out to me that the daytime view from the windows on the third floor of his home makes it look like he lives in the middle of a great forest. Trees are just everywhere; people are nowhere to be found. But at night, when the lights of human life emerge, the windows reveal that he does indeed live in a big city. Fremont and Ballard are actually dense, urban neighborhoods, but this fact can only be seen after night falls. And the city is there until sunrise, at which point it vanishes like some vampire. After the visit, as I walked to a nearby bus stop that was beneath a streetlamp and a clear sky with a few cold stars, it occurred to me that something similar must happen with the view astronauts have of our planet from space. During the day, Earth is all nature—green forests, blue seas, brown deserts, white mountaintops and clouds. But when the sun goes, nature goes with it, and the only thing one can see is the planet of apes.

On another night—this time in 2008, and this time we ordered pizza—he said to me the most curious thing. We were talking about sleep and dreams and death. I told him that dreams were the only place I saw my mother, who had been dead since 2003 and is now buried on a hill in Renton. She originally came from the hills of Manicaland, which is in eastern Zimbabwe, next to the border with Mozambique. I told him that these dream encounters were strange because it seemed my mother had somehow survived her terminal illness, that somehow the doctor's prediction (six months to live) was wrong. She had more than five years to live. She could even live longer than that. But she was still so frail, still about to die, still sitting in the sunlight that fell from the skylight in our Central District duplex. (This was our last home as a family; the middle one was on 36 Dover Road in Harare, the capital of Zimbabwe, and the first one was somewhere in Redcliff, also in Zimbabwe.) I always have to be gentle with my mother in my dreams. Raban, caressing with the tips of his fingers the stem of a wineglass, then told me that all of his dreams occur in England. "All of them?" I asked, looking at his face for a hint of mischief. I found nothing of the sort. He was very serious. He only dreams of a country he has not lived in for twenty years.

Raban moved to Seattle in 1991, after first visiting the city in 1988, when he stayed at the Josephinum building on Second and Stewart and was impressed with the city's signs for adult businesses. (All of this is captured in his book *Hunting Mister Heartbreak*.) He has a daughter here. A boat here. A home here. And a failed marriage. But when he turns out the light beside his bed and falls asleep, he leaves this real world behind and returns to his old world of England—to its villages, its rivers, its ships, its pubs, its laughter. (The rural images just listed have more to do with me than Raban, who is really an urban creature, a man of the town.) But is this not the true condition or a writer? This kind of exile? Your body is here in a foreign land, but your whole mind never really leaves where you're from. But I never dream of Zimbabwe.

Whenever it's time to go, it's always abrupt. While in the middle of a complicated conversation (something about a new book that everyone is talking about, about a big story that's all over the news, about recent events or scandals in local and national politics), Raban suddenly says: "Listen, Charles, I need to close shop. We will have to continue the discussion at another time." At that point, I realize how late it is and how tired he looks, and feel bad for being so inconsiderate. I always ask to help clean the mess I helped make. He always says no. He will take care of it later. I finish what remains in my wineglass, look out at the big city in the windows, stand from the table, thank him for being a great host, and leave the room that looks and feels like the cabin of a ship. What journey is this great writer on?

KELLY FROH

Co-Founder and Co-Organizer, Short Run Seattle Comix & Arts Festival

HOW THE SHORT RUN FESTIVAL CAME TO BE

For years, we heard people grumble about how Brooklyn, Chicago, Portland, and even Olympia had comic-art festivals that focused on self-publishers and how all Seattle had were large conventions that didn't "get" them. So many people seemed to want a new festival, but no one was making it happen. We were a little naive about how much work it would take to put one together, but I'm glad we were—if we'd had any idea what we were getting into we might not have done it at all. As artists ourselves, we knew what kind of festival we would want to attend, and that's what we have tried to build and see grow. Our curated festival features self-publishers, micropublishers, artists, and authors from around the world making incredible books by hand, in small batches. These are art objects as well as books.

THE ONE BOOK BY A SEATTLEITE TO PUT IN THE HANDS OF A VISITOR

I'd insist on a Jim Woodring graphic novel, maybe *Congress of the Animals* or *Weathercraft*. Jim is an artist who has created his own world and his own language, and it's a privilege to lose yourself in one of his beautiful books.

SEATTLE GRAPHIC NOVELIST WHO DESERVES MORE ATTENTION

Once again, I need to mention Jim Woodring, who should be getting flown all over the world more often to present his work and pick up his awards. Also, Bruce Bickford, the amazing artist and animator who I fear will be in insolation in SeaTac without one more hurray, only because he is so engrossed in his work that he can't bring a project to a close. I also believe my partner, artist Eroyn Franklin, needs to have a book publisher that will give her all the resources to make the books she wants to make; they would not be disappointed. I sit and wonder what my friend Stacey Levine could produce if she didn't also have to teach and do other things. Her stories are so sharp and shocking to me that I am left exhausted and looking up words I didn't know that I now want to use every day.

BEST NEIGHBORHOOD TO SET A MURDER MYSTERY

Definitely Georgetown. It has a dark-alley brusqueness about it. As often as I've been there, I still feel like there's a lot I don't know or can't see. I love it because it feels rougher than other Seattle neighborhoods, which is an exciting feeling.

NEIGHBORHOOD BOOKSTORE OF CHOICE

I visit the Elliott Bay Book Company for almost every literary need, but I also try to buy my graphic novels and comics from Zanadu downtown, or Fantagraphics Bookstore & Gallery in Georgetown, because I would really be upset if these places went out of business. Zanadu is the shop that typifies "comic-book store," with product reaching to the ceiling and cardboard superheroes welcoming you in the window, but it also reaches beyond with new "indie" and "local" sections. Fantagraphics Bookstore is a cultural hub, where cartoonists come to meet their visiting idols and peruse a tightly curated selection of the world's best graphic novels and comic books. Larry Reid puts on great shows there, supports local comic artists, gets people excited about buying comics, and is truly the beating heart of that store.

BEST DAY JOB FOR A WRITER IN SEATTLE

If the writer can deal with interruptions, and starting and stopping a lot, a lazy office job is great. You are always staring at a screen anyway; no one needs to know what exactly you are typing.

AFTERWORD

BY PAUL CONSTANT

You can cherry-pick the Internet for confirmation of any terrible worldview you want, of course, but bear with me for a moment. Here's the beginning of a one-star customer book review of *Moby-Dick* from Amazon:

"My Kindle version has Moby Dick actually entering the fray 95% into the book. What a waste of time . . ."

It's hard to remember in this age of vapid fill-in-the-star online "reviewing" and drive-by commenting by oblivious narcissists like the Amazon customer quoted above, but literary criticism is an especially privileged art form. Book reviewing is the only form of criticism done in the same medium as the art being critiqued. That is to say, nobody designs a building as a critique of another architect's work. Nobody dances a review of a dance performance. I have never once seen an art critic take up palette and brush to paint a nuanced critical response to a painting.

We book reviewers respond to words with words. Think about that. We create pieces of literature in direct response to literature! That's a special, sacred, and intimidating trust. A poorly written book review is about as useful as a fishnet condom; if a reviewer can't demonstrate a basic understanding of structure and metaphor and other standard techniques of written communication, how can we trust him to understand how to read a piece of writing? Read enough book reviews and you'll eventually come across a few that are more artful pieces of literature than the book being reviewed. Those moments always take my breath away with their specialness, like a lively rap battle or a career-ending gaffe in a political debate.

By now you've read all about the diverse strengths and unique minds of Seattle's vivacious literary scene. Ryan Boudinot asked me to write a review of the book that would be published in the back of the book I'm reviewing, a terrific idea that I've never seen done before. And my review is coming, but first I have the unfortunate responsibility to inform you that of Seattle's many literary strengths, artful book reviews are not one of them. Maybe it's because we're home to Amazon, which has spawned more shitty book reviews than any other force in the history of the universe, but more likely it's because our local media scene has been on life support since the turn of the century.

Let me lay out the book reviewing scene in Seattle as it stands in late 2014, at the time of this writing: My name is Paul Constant, and I am a full-time paid book reviewer for the Seattle-based alternative weekly the *Stranger*. (Nice to meet you.) I've reviewed hundreds of books for my paper, and my reviews are published every Wednesday in the print edition, with even more published online every week at thestranger.com/books. The other full-time book review editor in town is Mary Ann Gwinn, who works at the *Seattle Times* and employs a small team of free-lancers, whose book reviews are published in the paper a few times a week.

That's it.

It's just Mary Ann and me sitting in a leaky media lifeboat, staring awkwardly at each other as the Google-colored sharks circle ever closer. (There's one revolver and one bullet in the center of the boat. Who's going to lunge for them first?) Sure, the *Seattle Weekly* technically employs an arts editor who is supposed to cover books along with visual arts and theater, but it maybe runs three or four book reviews a year, maximum. *City Arts*, too, will occasionally blow out an interview with an author into a cover story once or twice a year. But part of the value of book reviewing is the regu-larity of it, the diary of a reading life doled out in regular install-ments, sprinkled with gossipy accounts of what happened at a few of the dozens of readings happening around town every week. If you want to learn what's happening in Seattle's literary scene, you more or less have two options: Mary Ann and me.

That's it.

I wish we had more competition. I'd love it if some upstart kid launched a Seattle-centric literary review blog with all her book-minded friends. I'd look forward to reading her blog every single damn day. I'd be overjoyed if other media outlets in town realized that even though a book review section often doesn't pay for itself in advertising dollars, it is a necessary component if you want to truly cover the depth and breadth of Seattle's arts scene. But they haven't realized that, and they're not likely going to. So if you want to know what's happening with books in Seattle, you only have two choices for your news. Sorry about that. (Here's the part where I suck up to my bosses, Christopher Frizzelle, the editor in chief and former books editor at the *Stranger*, and Tim Keck, the publisher. They've been unwavering in their support of books coverage for the paper, even at times when I'm sure it would have made smarter financial sense to smother my book section in its crib. Thank you, gentlemen. I wish there were a dozen more of you in Seattle; we'd all be healthier for it.)

Anyway, where was I? Oh, yeah: I was going to review this book.

THE BOOK CLUB

Seattle City of Literature Is a Sprawling, Ambitious, Personal
Account of Literary Seattle

by Paul Constant

As Ryan Boudinot hints in the thrilling introduction to his new anthology *Seattle: City of Literature* (Sasquatch Books, $19.95), Seattle has always demonstrated an inferiority complex when compared to New York and Los Angeles and San Francisco and other major American cities. And for good reason! For decades, we saw the best artistic minds of our city spirited away as if by assembly line to find their fortune elsewhere. But now things have changed—Boudinot credits the Internet, although presumably our booming economy also has something to do with it—and finally our geniuses are staying put, planting their flags in Seattle and saying, "This is who I am." It's a powerful moment in Seattle's history, a tectonic event that is shaping the city, presumably, for the better. *Seattle* is intended as a snapshot of Seattle at this moment, and also as a patchwork history of the city in those awkward high school years, when we were figuring out who we are.

Seattle divides its essays into five sections ("Remembering," "Learning," "Working," "Performing," and "Reflecting") written by a cross-section of the city's talent: poets, memoirists, novelists, booksellers, and the nonprofit support staff that keeps food on the tables of authors as they try to wrestle something meaningful and lasting out of unemployment. It's a nicely gossipy book—many in the literary community have heard variations of some of these stories over tables crowded with empty beer pitchers for decades now—and it's slanted toward the positive, more of a proud showcase than a ribald tell-all.

But that's okay. The best parts of this book have captured pieces of Seattle literary history that otherwise might have completely disappeared into the rafters of bars. Consider the group history of the Typing Explosion, a "girl band with writers instead of musicians" that already feels like a fond-but-evaporating memory. Like everyone who has attended a Typing Explosion show, I have friendly memories of clicking and clacking and Jackie O clothing wedged firmly into the folds of my brain. But brains are a notoriously iffy storage medium—they don't have the heft or the reliability, say, of the hard drive purring like a kitten underneath my desktop right now—and what *Seattle* says in chapters like this is important: We were here. We mattered.

Much like the city this book honors, *Seattle* is shot through with surprising bursts of almost-impossible beauty. You won't find much stylistically in common between Elissa Washuta's gorgeous millennia-spanning salvo that opens the book and Tom Robbins's gossipy reminiscences of a time not so long gone by, but you can surely appreciate them both as excellent pieces of writing. Kathleen Alcalá relays the secret history of Seattle's underappreciated science-fiction roots, brilliantly, with an anecdote about a fainting spell. You can smell the stale beer oozing out of the flesh of Karen Finneyfrock's account of Seattle's booming poetry slam scene. Doug Nufer's explanation of how Oulipo discovered Seattle is a missing link between Georges Perec and Seattle's thriving, constraint-happy young poetry scene. My *Stranger* colleague Charles Mudede beautifully pays tribute to Jonathan Raban, one of the brightest literary lights ever to crash-land in this city. These are all rare gems, and without an ambitious book like *Seattle*, they may never have been fully excavated.

And *Seattle* is interspersed with quick magazine-like personality profiles featuring those in the scene who maybe don't get the microphone as often as they should: booksellers, venue bookers, zine librarians. An eager reader might skip right over these questionnaires in order to get to the meatier essays, but that would be a mistake; read all together, these profiles accrue into a portrait of Seattle's variegated tastes. (They also prove we may discover our joy in different places, but the one thing we can all agree on as a city, it seems, is that Sherman Alexie is the best performer in town.)

Of course, pieces of *Seattle* could use some improvement. I would have preferred more works of journalism and intensive research,

for example, spread throughout the book, rather than a menag-
erie of recollections. But on the whole, it's an impressive feat. Like
any night at the bar, this could've devolved into a mess, with too
much bragging, score-settling, and mansplaining. Credit has to go
to Boudinot for doing the hard (invisible) work of arranging the
bustling cacophony of these authors into a disciplined symphony
orchestra. (And you have to respect *Seattle* at the very least as the
only book in the world that could place Garth Stein, the author of
a blockbuster global best seller about a talking dog, immediately
next to Stacey Levine, the impeccable genius who writes challenging, masterful short fiction. If Levine and Stein were to ever shake
hands, the proximity of brilliant artistry and mass-market senti-
mentality would likely create a frisson of matter and antimatter
whose collision would likely destroy the universe. Good thing that
experiment of weird literary science occurs only safely between
these two covers.)

It's unorthodox for a reviewer to do this, but I'd like to make
an addendum to one of the stories in *Seattle*. Tom Nissley, in his
account of David Foster Wallace's reading at Elliott Bay Book
Company from *Infinite Jest* writes:

> As I remember it, he left the podium and was met halfway by
> the bookseller who had introduced him, and who reminded
> him that there was also to be an audience Q&A. He wasn't
> thrilled about the idea, and for an uncomfortable moment
> they stood there, neither on the stage nor off it, until some-
> one threw out a question from the crowd, to which Wallace

said, "If that's what they're going to be like, I don't think so." And that was that.

Nissley unfortunately leaves out the best part of this story. I wasn't there, but I have confirmed with two booksellers in attendance that the question asked of Wallace was the one that nearly every novelist dreads: "Where do your ideas come from?" It was such a stupid, innocent question that it knocked Wallace back on his heels. He apparently couldn't tell if it was ironic or not, and so he decided to respond harshly.

No Seattle author would have difficulty with this question; they understand where their ideas come from. The literary forces in this town—and yes, I'm going to be arrogant enough to include book reviewers in this category—know the source of our formidable power. For better and for worse, our inspiration is Seattle, the city all around us, in all its maddening glory. We believe in this city, and this city believes in us. Seattle proves conclusively that there's no better place on earth to be a lover of words.

That's my review. Now go write your own. Make it good.

Editor's Note:
Since writing this afterword, Paul Constant has left the Stranger. No word on whether Mary Ann Gwinn is feasting on his corpse.

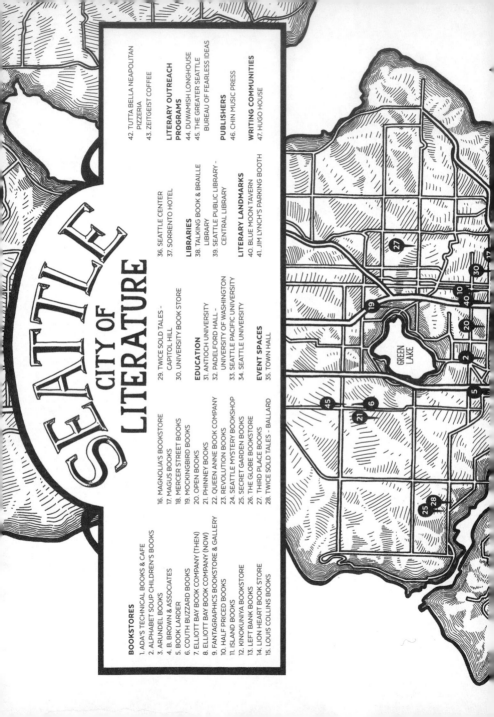

SEATTLE
CITY OF LITERATURE

BOOKSTORES

1. ADA'S TECHNICAL BOOKS & CAFE
2. ALPHABET SOUP CHILDREN'S BOOKS
3. ARUNDEL BOOKS
4. B. BROWN & ASSOCIATES
5. BOOK LARDER
6. COUTH BUZZARD BOOKS
7. ELLIOTT BAY BOOK COMPANY (THEN)
8. ELLIOTT BAY BOOK COMPANY (NOW)
9. FANTAGRAPHICS BOOKSTORE & GALLERY
10. HALF PRICED BOOKS
11. ISLAND BOOKS
12. KINOKUNIYA BOOKSTORE
13. LEFT BANK BOOKS
14. LION HEART BOOK STORE
15. LOUIS COLLINS BOOKS
16. MAGNOLIA'S BOOKSTORE
17. MAGUS BOOKS
18. MERCER STREET BOOKS
19. MOCKINGBIRD BOOKS
20. OPEN BOOKS
21. PHINNEY BOOKS
22. QUEEN ANNE BOOK COMPANY
23. REVOLUTION BOOKS
24. SEATTLE MYSTERY BOOKSHOP
25. SECRET GARDEN BOOKS
26. THE GLOBE BOOKSTORE
27. THIRD PLACE BOOKS
28. TWICE SOLD TALES - BALLARD
29. TWICE SOLD TALES -
    CAPITOL HILL
30. UNIVERSITY BOOK STORE

EDUCATION

31. ANTIOCH UNIVERSITY
32. PADELFORD HALL -
    UNIVERSITY OF WASHINGTON
33. SEATTLE PACIFIC UNIVERSITY
34. SEATTLE UNIVERSITY

EVENT SPACES

35. TOWN HALL
36. SEATTLE CENTER
37. SORRENTO HOTEL

LIBRARIES

38. TALKING BOOK & BRAILLE
    LIBRARY
39. SEATTLE PUBLIC LIBRARY -
    CENTRAL LIBRARY

LITERARY LANDMARKS

40. BLUE MOON TAVERN
41. JIM LYNCH'S PARKING BOOTH
42. TUTTA BELLA NEAPOLITAN
    PIZZERIA
43. ZEITGEIST COFFEE

LITERARY OUTREACH PROGRAMS

44. DUWAMISH LONGHOUSE
45. THE GREATER SEATTLE
    BUREAU OF FEARLESS IDEAS

PUBLISHERS

46. CHIN MUSIC PRESS

WRITING COMMUNITIES

47. HUGO HOUSE

GREEN LAKE

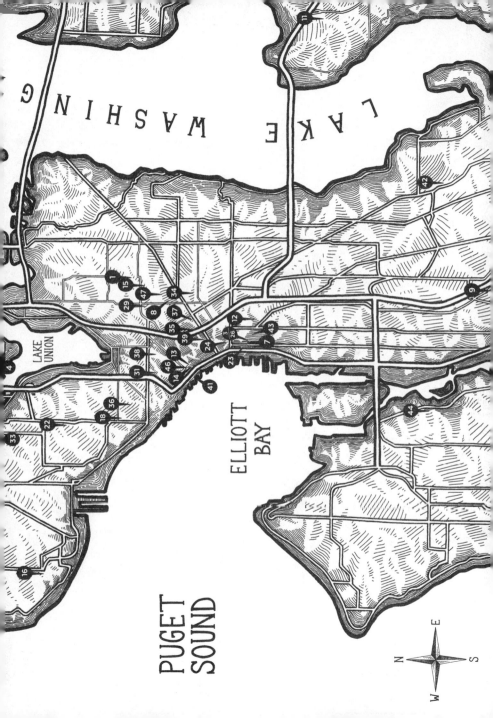

INVENTORY

BOOKSTORES

Ada's Technical Books and Cafe: *seattletechnicalbooks.com*

Alphabet Soup Children's Books: *alphabetsoupchildrensbooks.blogspot.com*

Arundel Books: *arundelbookstores.com*

B. Brown and Associates: *bbrownandassoc.com*

Book Larder: *booklarder.com*

Couth Buzzard Books: *buonobuzzard.com*

East West Bookshop: *eastwestbookshop.com*

Elliott Bay Book Company: *elliottbaybook.com*

Island Books: *mercerislandbooks.com*

Kinokuniya Bookstore: *kinokuniya.com*

Left Bank Books: *leftbankbooks.com*

Louis Collins Books: *collinsbooks.com*

Magnolia's Bookstore: *magnoliasbookstore.com*

Magus Books: *magusbooksseattle.com*

Mercer Street Books: *mercerstreetusedbooks.com*

Mockingbird Books: *mockingbirdbooksgl.com*

Nudelman Rare Books: *nudelmanbooks.com*

Open Books: *openpoetrybooks.com*

Phinney Books: *phinneybooks.com*

Queen Anne Book Company: *qabookco.com*

Revolution Books: *revolutionbookssea.org*

Santoro's Books: *santorosbooks.com*

Seattle Mystery Bookshop: *seattlemystery.com*

Secret Garden Books: *secretgardenbooks.com*

Third Place Books: *thirdplacebooks.com*

Twice Sold Tales: *twicesoldtales.info*

University Book Store: *bookstore.washington.edu*

PUBLISHERS

alice blue books: *etsy.com/shop/alicebluebooks*

Aqueduct Press: *aqueductpress.com*

Black Heron Press: *blackheronpress.com*

Chin Music Press: *chinmusicpress.com*

Dock Street Press: *dockstreetpress.com*

Fantagraphics: *fantagraphics.com*

Floating Bridge Press: *floatingbridgepress.org*

Fuzzy Hedgehog Press: *fuzzyhedgehogpress.com*

Jaded Ibis Press: *jadedibisproductions.com*

Marquand Books: *marquandbooks.com*

Mountaineers Books: *mountaineersbooks.org*

Ravenna Press: *ravennapress.com/books*

Sasquatch Books: *sasquatchbooks.com*

University of Washington Press: *washington.edu/uwpress*

Wave Books: *wavepoetry.com*

JOURNALS & MAGAZINES

alice blue review: alicebluereview.org

Big Fiction: bigfictionmagazine.com

Floating Bridge Review: floatingbridgepress.org/fb-review

Monarch Review: themonarchreview.org

Moss: mosslit.com

Pacifica: pacificareview.com

Poetry Northwest: poetrynw.org

Raven Chronicles: ravenchronicles.org

The Intruder Comics Newspaper: intrudercomics.tumblr.com

The James Franco Review: thejamesfrancoreview.com

The Seattle Review: theseattlereview.org

The Stranger: thestranger.com

LITERARY COMMUNITY OUTREACH PROGRAMS

Duwamish Longhouse: *duwamishtribe.org/longhouse*

First Book: *firstbook.org*

Friends of the Seattle Public Library: *friendsofspl.org*

Literacy Council of Seattle: *literacyseattle.org*

Pongo Teen Writing: *pongoteenwriting.org/index.php*

Seattle7Writers: *seattle7writers.org*

Team Read: *teamread.org*

The Greater Seattle Bureau of Fearless Ideas: *fearlessideas.org*

WRITING COMMUNITIES/NETWORKS

African American Writers Association: *aawa-seattle.com*

Book Club of Washington: *bookclubofwashington.sharepoint.com*

Hugo House: *hugohouse.org*

NaNoWriMo Seattle: *nanowrimo.org/regions/usa-washington-seattle*

Northwest Independent Editors Guild: *edsguild.org*

Pacific Northwest Booksellers Association: *pnba.org*

Pacific Northwest Writers Association: *pnwa.org*

Seattle Free Lances: *seattlefreelances.org*

Seattle Poetry Gathering: *seattlepoet.blogspot.com*

Society of Children's Book Writers and Illustrators: Western Washington: *scbwi.org*

Seattle Poetics LAB (SPLAB): *splab.org*

Women's National Book Association, Seattle Chapter: *wnba-seattlechapter.org*

WRITING CLASSES, CONFERENCES & RETREATS

Clarion West Writer's Workshop: *clarionwest.org*

Hedgebrook: *hedgebrook.org*

Path with Art: *pathwithart.org*

Puget Sound Writing Project: *depts.washington.edu/pswpuw*

The Writer's Workshop: *thewritersworkshop.net*

COLLEGE & UNIVERSITY WRITING PROGRAMS

Antioch University Arts & Literature program: *antiochseattle.edu/academics-ausea/ ba-degree-completion-liberal-studies-2/arts-literature*

University of Washington Bothell MFA in Creative Writing & Poetics: *uwb.edu/mfa*

Seattle University Creative Writing program: *seattleu.edu/artsci/departments/english/creativewriting*

Seattle University Writing Studies Minor program: *seattleu.edu/artsci/english/writing-studies*

Seattle Pacific University Creative Writing Minor program: *spu.edu/depts/english*

Seattle Pacific University Low-Residency MFA in Creative Writing: *spu.edu/prospects/grad/Academics/MFA*

Seattle Pacific University Professional Writing Minor program: *spu.edu/depts/english*

University of Washington Continuing & Professional Education: *pce.uw.edu/explore-programs.aspx*

University of Washington Creative Writing program:
depts.washington.edu/engl/cw

LIBRARIES

Antioch University Library: *antiochseattle.edu/library*

King County Library System: *kcls.org*

Little Free Libraries: *littlefreelibrary.org*

Seattle University Lemieux Library and McGoldrick Learning
Commons: *seattleu.edu/library*

Seattle Pacific University Library: *spu.edu/library*

Talking Book and Braille Library: *wtbbl.org*

The Seattle Public Library: *spl.org*

University of Washington Suzzallo Library:
lib.washington.edu/suzzallo

EVENTS & FESTIVALS

APRIL Festival: *aprilfestival.com*

Book-It Repertory Theater: *book-it.org*

Debut Lit: *debutlit.wordpress.com*

Lit Crawl: *litcrawl.org/seattle*

Seattle Antiquarian Book Fair: *seattlebookfair.com*

Seattle Arts & Lectures: *lectures.org*

Short Run Comix & Arts Festival: *shortrun.org*

Subtext Reading Series: *users.speakeasy.net/~subtext*

The Gardner Center for Asian Art and Ideas: *seattleartmuseum.org/ gardnercenter*

Town Hall: *townhallseattle.org*

LITERARY AGENCIES

Anne Depue

Wales Literary Agency, Inc.: *waleslit.com*

MARKETING & PUBLICITY FIRMS

Alice Acheson Agency: *sites.google.com/site/alicebacheson*

CLS Communications: *clsbooks.com/about*

Visit Seattle: *visitseattle.org/Home.aspx*

LITERARY WEBSITES, BLOGS & APPS

Book Patrol: *bookpatrol.net*

BooksILove.com: *booksilove.com*

Northwest Book Lovers: *nwbooklovers.org/about-us*

Shelf Awareness: *shelf-awareness.com*

The Zine Project Seattle: *zineprojectseattle.wordpress.com*

OTHER LITERARY ORGANIZATIONS

Babel/Salvage: *babelsalvage.com*

Bushwick Book Club: *thebushwickbookclubseattle.com*

Girl Friday Productions: *girlfridayproductions.com*

Jack Straw Cultural Center: *jackstraw.org*

Nancy Pearl: *nancypearl.com*

Old Growth Northwest: *oldgrowthnw.org*

Seattle City of Literature: *seattlecityoflit.org*

Sorrento Hotel: *hotelsorrento.com*

The Business of Books with Jen and Kerry:
bizofbooks.wordpress.com

Two Pens: *twopens.com*

Washington Center for the Book:
spl.org/about-the-library/leaders-and-organizations/
washington-center-for-the-book-at-the-seattle-public-library

Youth Speaks Seattle: *youthspeaks206.tumblr.com*

Zine Archive & Publishing Project (ZAPP): *zappseattle.org*

CONTRIBUTORS

RYAN BOUDINOT is the author of *The Octopus Rises, Blueprints of the Afterlife, Misconception,* and *The Littlest Hitler.* He is founder of Seattle City of Literature. For more information, visit seattlecityoflit.org.

KATHLEEN ALCALÁ is the author of *Mrs. Vargas and the Dead Naturalist, Spirits of the Ordinary, The Flower in the Skull,* and *Treasures in Heaven,* all fiction about the southwest and Mexico. Her collection of essays is called *The Desert Remembers My Name: On Family and Writing.* Her work has received the Governor's Writers Award, the Washington State Book Award, the Western States Book Award, two Artist Trust Fellowships, and numerous other recognitions for which she is grateful. Alcalá teaches at the Northwest Institute of Literary Arts.

TARA ATKINSON is cofounder and managing director of APRIL and a writer. Her work has been published by alice blue books, the *Iowa Review* and *City Arts* magazine.

Currently the program director at Town Hall Seattle, **STESHA BRANDON** works with community and publishing partners to curate more than 200 events in Town Hall's Arts & Culture, Civics, and Seattle Science Lectures series. Prior to her work at Town Hall, Stesha was manager of Public Relations and Events at University Book Store for nearly ten years.

MATT BRIGGS is the author of eight works of fiction including *The Remains of River Names* and *The Strong Man*. His first novel, *Shoot the Buffalo*, was awarded an American Book Award by the Before Columbus Foundation.

REBECCA BROWN is the author of a dozen books published in the United States, abroad, and in translation. Titles include *The Gifts of the Body*, *The Dogs*, *The End of Youth*, and *American Romances*. She has also written for theater, dance opera, the visual arts, and solo performance, and has exhibited work in museums and galleries in the United States and Canada. Her criticism appears regularly in the *Stranger*. She cofounded, and was first curator of, the Jack Straw Writers Program, was the first writer-in-residence at Hugo House, and is a former director of the Port Townsend Writers' Conference. She has been awarded residencies at MacDowell, Yaddo, Centrum, The Millay Colony, etc. She is Senior Artist in Residence at the University of Washington, Bothell, and a senior faculty member at Goddard College, Vermont.

PAM CADY has been a bookseller since 1981. She has worked at the University Book Store for eighteen years and is the manager of the General Books Department.

DEB CALETTI is a National Book Award finalist, PEN USA finalist, winner of the Washington State Book Award, and author of more than twelve novels for young adults and adults including *Honey, Baby, Sweetheart*; *Stay*; *He's Gone*; and *The Secrets She Keeps*.

PAUL CONSTANT is the book review editor at the *Stranger*, an alternative weekly in Seattle. His writing has also appeared in *Newsweek*, the *Progressive*, *Utne Reader*, and alternative weeklies around North America.

KEVIN CRAFT is the editor of *Poetry Northwest*. His books include *Solar Prominence* and five volumes of the anthology *Mare Nostrum*, an annual collection of Italian translation and Mediterranean-inspired writing. He directs both the Written Arts Program at Everett Community College and the University of Washington's Creative Writing in Rome Program.

CHARLES R. CROSS is the author of nine books including *New York Times* best-selling biographies of Kurt Cobain, Heart, and Jimi Hendrix. *Heavier Than Heaven*, his Cobain biography, won the ASCAP Award for Outstanding Biography in 2002. Cross was editor of the *Rocket* from 1986 to 2000, and chronicled the rise of the Northwest scene during the heyday of grunge.

JAMES CROSSLEY has earned a living through one form of literary commerce or another since 1997. He is currently a frontline bookseller and blogger at Island Books.

CLAIRE DEDERER is the author of the best-selling memoir *Poser: My Life in Twenty-Three Yoga Poses*. She is a longtime contributor to the *New York Times* and has written essays, criticism, and reports for the *Atlantic*, *Vogue*, the *Nation*, *Slate*, and many other publications.

RUTH DICKEY is the author of a chapbook, *Paper Houses, Sky Ceilings*, and her poems and essays have appeared in *Alimentum*, the *Baltimore Review*, *Colere*, *Divide*, *ellipsis*, *Kalliope*, *Paper Street*, the *Potomac Review*, *roger*, *Slipstream*, *Sonora Review*, and others. Ruth holds an MFA from University of North Carolina, Greensboro, and has taught poetry workshops in a variety of nontraditional venues, including soup kitchens, drop-in centers, and the DC public schools. She has received a Mayor's Arts Award from Washington, DC, and an individual artist grant from the DC Commission and Arts and Humanities. She currently serves as the executive director of Seattle Arts & Lectures; learn more at www.lectures.org.

JONATHAN EVISON is the *New York Times* best-selling author of three award-winning novels: *All About Lulu*, *West of Here*, and *The Revised Fundamentals of Caregiving*, soon to be a major motion picture. Evison's fourth novel *This Is Your Life, Harriet Chance!* publishes in the fall of 2015.

KAREN FINNEYFROCK is the author of two novels, *The Sweet Revenge of Celia Door* and *Starbird Murphy and the World Outside*, and the poetry collection *Ceremony for the Choking Ghost*. She is an editor of the poetry anthology *Courage: Daring Poems for Gutsy Girls*.

WILLIE FITZGERALD is the cofounder and creative director of APRIL, a festival of small press and independent publishing held every year in Seattle. He grew up in Cabin John, MD, and went to school in Wisconsin.

KATHLEEN FLENNIKEN'S two poetry collections are *Famous* and *Plume*. She was the 2012–2014 Washington State Poet Laureate.

KELLY FROH is one third of the all-women organizing team that is Short Run Seattle. Eroyn Franklin, Janice Headley, and Froh are growing their four-year-old comics and arts festival into a year-round organization that spotlights small press artists. Future endeavors include a ladies' comics residency, a self-publishing grant program, skill shares, and more. Learn more at shortrun.org.

NICOLE HARDY is the author of the memoir *Confessions of a Latter-day Virgin* and the poetry collections *This Blonde* and *Mud Flap Girl's XX Guide to Facial Profiling.*

ELI HASTINGS is an author, father, and youth and family therapist living in metro Seattle with his nutcase toddler and big shot doctor wife. He's the author of *Falling Room* and the acclaimed *Clearly Now, the Rain: A Memoir of Love and Other Trips* as well as dozens of smaller publications. He serves clients at Changing Stories Counseling and is the assistant director of Pongo Teen Writing.

LESLEY HAZELTON is a veteran Middle East journalist whose work has appeared in the *New York Times*, *Esquire*, *Vanity Fair*, the *Nation*, and other publications. The author of several books on Middle East politics, religion, and history, she now lives in Seattle.

TERI HEIN is the founding executive director of The Greater Seattle Bureau of Fearless Ideas (formerly known an 826 Seattle). The organization has won numerous awards, including the National Arts and Humanities Youth Program Award, which Hein accepted from First Lady Michelle Obama in 2011. Hein has published numerous essays and stories, including her award-winning memoir *Atomic Farmgirl: The Betrayal of Chief Qualchan, the Appaloosa, and Me.*

SONORA JHA is the author of the novel *Foreign*. She is an associate professor of journalism and media studies at Seattle University. Her Op-Eds have appeared in the *New York Times*, the *Seattle Times*, and *Seattle Weekly*. She was formerly a journalist in India and Singapore and holds a PhD in political communication.

RACHEL KESSLER grew up in Seattle in the 1980s and currently lives a few blocks from the hospital in which she was born. Her work has been published in the anthology *The Open Daybook*, and she is co-author of books *Who Are We?* (plus seven-inch vinyl record) and *TYPO*, made as cofounder of collaborative literary performance teams the Vis-a-Vis Society and The Typing Explosion, respectively. She is the recipient of a Seattle City Artist award. She works as a teaching artist with Writers in the Schools, Path with Art, and Centrum.

BHARTI KIRCHNER is the author of five novels and four nonfiction works. She has won numerous awards for her writing, including a fellowship from Virginia Center for the Creative Arts. Her sixth novel, *Goddess of Fire*, a historical novel set in seventeenth-century India, will be released worldwide in late 2015.

STACEY LEVINE is the author of *The Girl with Brown Fur*, *Frances Johnson*, *Dra—*, and *My Horse and Other Stories*. Recipient of a PEN Fiction Award and a Stranger Genius Award for Literature, her work has appeared in *Fence*, *Tin House*, *Fairy Tale Review*, *Yeti*, and others. She is working on a third novel.

MIA LIPMAN is the principal editor and book reviewer at Dots & Dashes, cofounder of *Canteen* magazine, and host of the Lit Fix reading and music series. Learn more at dotdotdashes.com and litfixseattle.com.

All three of **JIM LYNCH'S** novels—*The Highest Tide*, *Border Songs*, and *Truth Like the Sun*—are set in the Northwest and were adapted to the stage. His honors include the Washington State Book Award.

FRANCES McCUE is the author of two books of poetry (*The Stenographer's Breakfast* and *The Bled*) and two books of prose (*The Car That Brought You Here Still Runs* and *Mary Randlett Portraits*). She was the founding director of Hugo House and is currently the Writer in Residence in the University Honors Program at UW.

BRIAN McGUIGAN's nonfiction has appeared in *Gawker*, *Salon*, The Rumpus, The Weeklings, and elsewhere, and he writes a monthly column on fatherhood called Daddy Issues for *ParentMap* magazine. He's the author of the poetry chapbook *More Than I Left Behind*.

PETER MOUNTFORD'S first novel, *A Young Man's Guide to Late Capitalism*, won the 2012 Washington State Book Award in fiction. His second novel, *The Dismal Science*, was a *New York Times* Editor's Choice. He is on faculty at Sierra Nevada's low-residency MFA, and is the event curator at Hugo House.

CHARLES MUDEDE is a Zimbabwean-born film critic, film-maker, and writer for the *Stranger*. Mudede collaborated with the director Robinson Devor on two films, *Police Beat* and *Zoo*, both of which premiered at Sundance—*Zoo* was screened at Cannes. Mudede has contributed to the *New York Times*, *LA Weekly*, the *Village Voice*, *Black Souls Journal*, *C Theory*, and *Cinema Scope*, and is on the editorial board for *ARCADE* magazine and the *Black Scholar*. Mudede has lived in Seattle since 1989.

SIERRA NELSON is author of *I Take Back the Sponge Cake*, made with visual artist Loren Erdrich, and chapbook *In Case of Loss*. She is a MacDowell Colony Fellow, a winner of the Carolyn Kizer Prize and CityArtist Grant from Seattle's Office of Arts & Culture, and a Pushcart Prize nominee. Her text-based installations, collaborative and solo, have appeared at the Frye Art Museum, Henry Art Gallery, the Seattle Aquarium, and SIM Gallery in Reykjavík, Iceland, and she has performed both nationally and internationally as cofounder of collaborative performance groups The Typing Explosion and the Vis-a-Vis Society. She teaches creative writing in Seattle, Friday Harbor, and Rome, Italy. Learn more at songsforsquid.tumblr.com.

TOM NISSLEY is the author of *A Reader's Book of Days*. A former books editor at Amazon.com, he is now the owner of Phinney Books in Seattle.

DOUG NUFER is the author of seven novels and three books of poetry, including *Never Again, Negativeland, By Kelman Out of Pessoa, We Were Werewolves*, and *The Dammed*. He often performs solo, with the word band Interrupture, and with musicians or dancers, indoors and in the wild.

SARAH PAUL OCAMPO is a writer, musician, and performer currently based in Seattle.

LARRY REID has served as director of Rosco Louie Gallery, Graven Image Gallery, and the Center on Contemporary Art (CoCA), and as curator for Experience Music Project (EMP) and Fantagraphics Books. He has co-authored several books including *Pop Surrealism: The Rise of Underground Art, Edward Colver: Blight at the End of the Funnel, Tiki Art Now!*, and *Sub Pop USA: The Subterranean Pop Music Anthology, 1980–1987*.

ERIC REYNOLDS is the associate publisher of Fantagraphics Books, where he has edited hundreds of books by the likes of Joe Sacco, Robert Crumb, Daniel Clowes, and many others over the past two decades.

TOM ROBBINS has been called "a vital natural resource" by the *Oregonian*, "one of the wildest and most entertaining novelists in the world" by the *Financial Times* of London, and "the most dangerous writer in the world today" by Fernanda Pivano of Italy's *Corriere della Sera*. A Southerner by birth, Robbins has lived in and around Seattle since 1962. Tom Robbins is mostly recognized for his novel *Even Cowgirls Get the Blues*, but he has also written eight more novels and many short stories and essays.

JUDITH ROCHE has won two American Book Awards, for editing *First Fish First People, Salmon Tales of the North Pacific*, and for the poetry collection *Wisdom of the Body*. A fourth poetry collection *All Fire All Water* is forthcoming. She has poems presented in several Seattle-area public art installations, and is widely published in magazines and journals. She is a fellow at the Black Earth Institute, an organization dedicated to social justice, environmental issues, and spiritual awareness.

BRUCE RUTLEDGE worked as a journalist in Japan for fifteen years before moving to Seattle to found Chin Music Press with his wife, Yuko Enomoto, in 2002. The press has been publishing engaging, beautiful, and affordable books ever since. Chin Music Press moved into Seattle's historic Pike Place Market in 2014.

JANIS SEGRESS, a poet and writer herself, appreciates a well-crafted book, no matter what genre. Janis buys the inventory for Queen Anne Book Company, so she has a voracious curiosity and wide range of interests, and is always searching to find what you and she both agree are the next great books.

MATTHEW SIMMONS is the author of the novella, *A Jello Horse* and two short story collections, *Happy Rock* and *The In-Betweens*, forthcoming. Learn more at matthewjsimmons.com.

RICK SIMONSON has worked at Seattle's Elliott Bay Book Company since 1976.

ROBERT SINDELAR has been a bookseller for over twenty-three years and is the managing partner of Third Place Books with two locations in the greater Seattle area. He is a current board member of the American Booksellers Association.

ED SKOOG is the author of two collections of poetry, *Mister Skylight* and *Rough Day*, which won the 2014 Washington State Book Award in poetry.

GARTH STEIN is the author of the *New York Times* best-selling novels *A Sudden Light* and *The Art of Racing in the Rain* as well as two earlier novels, *How Evan Broke His Head and Other Secrets* and *Raven Stole the Moon*. He is the cofounder of Seattle7Writers, a nonprofit collective of Pacific Northwest authors working to foster a passion for the written word.

TREE SWENSON cofounded Copper Canyon Press, where she worked for twenty years, serving as the executive director. She was then executive director of the Academy of American Poets, and has been the executive director at Hugo House since 2012.

EMILY VAN DER HARTEN is a musician, collage artist, and writer. She runs the Zine Archive and Publishing Project (ZAPP) with a few other enthusiastic folks devoted to cultural preservation and fostering creativity in everyone. ZAPP is an all-volunteer community archive devoted to preserving and providing radical accessibility to a collection of over thirty thousand zines. Her current ongoing project involves curating a zine, *Xenographic*, on behalf of ZAPP, which includes artists and authors based in Seattle and across the country.

ELISSA WASHUTA, a citizen of the Cowlitz Indian Tribe, is the author of the memoir *My Body Is a Book of Rules*. She serves as adviser for the department of American Indian Studies at the University of Washington and nonfiction faculty for the MFA program at the Institute of American Indian Arts.

SHAWN WONG is the author of two novels, *Homebase* and *American Knees*, and editor or co-editor of six anthologies including the landmark *Aiiieeeee! An Anthology of Asian American Writers*. *Americanese*, the film version of his novel *American Knees*, was released in 2013. He is a professor of Comparative Literature and English at the University of Washington.

BOOKS TO READ

....

....

....

....

....

....

....

....

....

....

....

....

....

....

....

....

....

SEATTLE AUTHORS TO READ

....

....

....

....

....

....

....

....

....

....

....

....

....

....

....

....

....

....

BOOKSTORES TO VISIT

....

....

....

....

....

....

....

....

....

....

....

....

....

....

....

....

EVENTS TO ATTEND

GROUPS AND ORGANIZATIONS TO JOIN

....

....

....

....

....

....

....

....

....

....

....

....

....

....

....

....

....

CLASSES TO TAKE

CONTRIBUTOR COPYRIGHTS

Seattle, Creative City © 2015 Ryan Boudinot

ESSAYS:

Elissa Washuta on Vi Hilbert © 2015 Elissa Washuta

Tom Robbins on His First Reading, Plate Glass, and More
© 2015 Tom Robbins

Jonathan Evison on Rock Music and (His Own) Bad Poetry
© 2015 Jonathan Evison

Deb Caletti on David Wagoner and the Long Haul © 2015 Deb Caletti

Tree Swenson on Carolyn Kizer © 2015 Tree Swenson

Ed Skoog on Peter Bagge, Open Books, Thom Jones, and *LitRag*
© 2015 Edward Skoog

Kathleen Alcalá on Tess Gallagher © 2015 Kathleen Alcalá

Matt Briggs on Discovering the Literature in His Own Backyard
© 2015 Matt Briggs

Kathleen Flenniken on Finding Her Community
© 2015 Kathleen Flenniken

Peter Mountford on David Shields © 2015 Peter Mountford

Claire Dederer on David Wagoner's Workshop © 2015 Claire Dederer

Kathleen Alcalá on Clarion West © 2015 Kathleen Alcalá

Tom Nissley on Marilynne Robinson, David Foster Wallace, Grant
Cogswell, and Coffee Shops © 2015 Tom Nissley

Eli Hastings on Pongo © 2015 Eli Hastings

Lesley Hazelton on Where She Writes © 2015 Lesley Hazelton